Treasury Investment Wisdom

Bernice Cohen

OB
ORION BUSINESS

To Joy
a very special sister

First published in Great Britain in 1999 by
Orion Business
An imprint of The Orion Publishing Group Ltd
Orion House, 5 Upper St Martin's Lane, London WC2H 9EA

A CIP catalogue record for this book is available from the British Library.

ISBN 0-75283-081-3

Designed and typeset by Ben Cracknell Studios

Printed and bound in Great Britain

Contents

••••••••••••••••••

Introduction

Around the world, collecting is a national pastime. The immensely popular BBC television 'Antiques Roadshow', now in its twenty-second year of continuous programmes, is testament to that. People and magpies share this common trait: they are attracted by rare or eye-catching objects. Drawn by some special effect or qualities, they pick up interesting items and carry them off to a safe place. Yet collecting unusual objects is a hobby as old as mankind. Archaeologists in Africa found a pebble on a living floor several hundred miles away from the nearest site where such pebbles occur naturally. The living floor was over a million years old and the conclusion is inescapable: the pebble must have been deliberately brought there by one of our enterprising early ancestors.

Pebble collecting sounds rather eccentric until you realise that Chinese and Japanese gardeners have used pebbles as a central feature of their designs for centuries; a fashion now being widely copied in the West. I don't collect pebbles, although I must confess, I did when I was younger, but then, I've collected a whole host of oddities over the years, because I am an incurable hoarder. Yet although I have only been collecting my investment quotations for nine years, as with every collection, the fascination of the search and the excitement of the finds are a source of endless pleasure.

There are some little books on maxims by investment gurus but I do not think there is a book that treats investment as a stand-alone topic for quotations. Many treasuries include just a couple of odd quotes on money or wealth, but nothing more. Yet investment quotations can be a rich source of guidance to investors searching for direction or new stimulation. Initially, my investment quotes grew as a spin-off from my reading of books on how to make a great success of increasing my wealth by investing. I made brief notes of interesting ideas or thoughts, gleaned during my reading sessions. The notes evolved into what I used to call my 'investment one-liners'. At first, I simply collected these helpful pithy phrases to implant useful ideas more firmly in my mind, especially when I was steeped in a bad mood over mistakes or getting things wrong. But later, I began collecting the quotes as morale boosters in their own right, adding to them incessantly, just as others collect beer mats or books, dolls or doilies.

While I revelled in the collecting, even then, I did not appreciate the true value of my growing treasury. After all, they are simply a group of popular catch-phrases, with no monetary worth. What I failed to recognise until much later, was their hidden value—the notion that as a cluster of pertinent sayings, mainly by knowledgeable investment gurus, they distil out the essence of wisdom from a group of brilliant people in the know. In bulk, the quotes add motivational and inspirational spice to the difficult task private investors face when making their assets grow.

There is undoubtedly an element of loneliness for small investors, working alone from home. Reading a good investment book on how a revered sage made his millions can help to dispel the gloom. You are never alone when you are reading as you establish a one to one contact with the author. This is a very precious link. But having a condensed assembly of wise sayings from a whole army of sages must be even better.

When I hit a bad patch or find I am holding a share that is showing a loss, my confidence ebbs away. It is then that I turn to my collection of quotes looking for one special item, one clever turn of phrase that will spark a good reaction and lift my sagging spirits. Many skills can be improved with motivational help: selling skills in a wide range of industries rely on inspirational boosters to give an added impetus to tired troops. There are relaxation tapes and exercises, hypnosis tapes or sessions and videos on a hundred different ways to improve your selling skills. Interestingly, I have always thought selling shares at the right time is an even more tricky skill to master than buying at the right time, so these inspirational messages do have a wide relevance.

I now think you will go a long way before you find a motivational booster as useful and flexible as a treasury of good investment quotations. With my swelling collection, I decided to include some of my own, home-grown favourites in *The Armchair Investor*, hoping to impart their energising properties to readers. Quotes have now become an integral part of all my subsequent books on investment and personal finance. They are even used on a daily basis as 'Financial Thought for the Day' on the mrscohen.com web site. The collection is now so large the next natural step, to publish them, seemed almost an inevitable follow-on from there. They are little nuggets of investment wisdom. A timely thought or idea captured succinctly in a mini-sentence or phrase. Easy to remember and inspirational when events turn bleak and nothing is going as you planned.

As this *Treasury* is dedicated exclusively to investment quotes, perhaps the first of its kind, I am delighted that Orion have decided the time is right to fill this gap in the library of discerning investors and give them their own portable treasury of investment wisdom. There are a few empty pages at the back of the *Treasury* for you to select some of your own favourites from the collection assembled here. You may even decide to start your very own unique collection. As I said right at the start, collecting is a world-wide human pastime, and the way most people begin is usually to be spurred into action by examining a ready established collection. Here, then, is part of mine, and I hope you become an addict, so you can add to the huge databank of pure investment quotations.

Naturally, you wouldn't expect me to write an introduction to this treasury without including at least one quote, so here, in conclusion, is a gem from that master of investment technique, Peter Lynch. He is a brilliant role model for private investors and an indefatigable expositor of succinct maxims that always seem to capture exactly the right mood, whatever the occasion:

'If I have a dollar and give it to you, between us we still have only one dollar. But if I give you an idea, we *both* have an idea.'

Guidance from Gurus

....

This *Treasury of Investment Wisdom* encompasses quotations by that super league of successful investors, affectionately dubbed gurus. Among academics, a popular theory claims the stock market is efficient: no one can make extraordinary gains because all the important facts are already priced into the market. They think the law of averages accounts for the fact that there are some successful investors, just as there are bound to be some losers. Few seriously wealthy investors have any kind words to say about this notion. They refute the possibility that the law of averages separates them from the losers. When we read what gurus say about the enormous range of skills and techniques they have mastered to turn themselves into winners, we might agree with them that the law of averages seems hopelessly irrelevant.

I personally do not see how such a highly emotive area as stock market investing can possibly be efficient. The whole basis of this activity rests entirely on mass human behaviour when it is being constantly subjected to an onslaught of unexpected news or events. Even in more tranquil conditions, human behaviour can be notoriously unpredictable or highly-strung. Collectively, people who put their money into the market are subject to abrupt and extreme mood swings that can border on the manic.

Observers witness outrageous over-exuberance and plunges into the depths of deepest panic, almost in equal measure.

Moreover, the underlying premise of efficiency looks puzzling. Professional investors dominate all other market participants. Their buy and sell activities drive prices and hence set the levels of the benchmark indices. If the law of averages was at work we might expect most professional performances to bunch around the average as represented by those benchmark indices. Yet what we find in practice is that over eighty per cent of professional fund managers underperform the indices against which they measure their progress. Performance statistics for outright speculators and market traders show the losers amount to an astonishing ninety-seven per cent. Pure speculation is a pursuit where grim determination, terrier-like persistence, tunnel-vision discipline and an iron nerve are mandatory for success. Such characteristics seem meaningless in the context of the law of averages.

In my opinion it is not the law of averages that creates the winners, but the decision by some participants that they will do whatever it takes to succeed. And what does it take? Without a doubt, it takes plenty of hard work and a modicum of good luck. Thomas Edison, inventor of the phonograph and the electric light bulb, was surely on the right track when he said, 'Genius is one per cent inspiration and ninety-nine per cent perspiration.'

I do not know if efficient markets academics test their own theories for personally acquiring wealth. However, the gurus do this every day. What they think therefore is highly pertinent, as they have polished their skills in the tough school of experience. This is where all the emotive action is played out. If we want to harvest some of their expertise, we should pay attention to what they have to say.

The Layout of the *Treasury*

Investment expertise is a compendium skill with many facets. The quotations have therefore been assembled into twelve over-arching themes. Although some of these are complete in themselves, for others there are several related sections that are pre-eminently relevant. At the back of the book some blank pages are included so you can begin collecting any quotations you happen to find which attract your interest, assuming you catch the collecting bug.

In every theme the sayings of the gurus come first, presented, where possible, in alphabetical order. They are followed by quotations from authors of investment books written by the active gurus who have penned accounts of their unique experiences and systems. These are then followed by professional fund manager quotations, and subsequently, there are quotations by authors who have compiled accounts of the views and expertise of one or many other successful investors. Most prominent here are books that I have personally read and books arranged as a series of interviews with top investors or traders. The next group of quotations listed covers the financial journalists who spend their working days analysing and commenting upon the major financial issues and personalities of the age. I consider their quotations to be hugely valuable because they put a lifetime of experience into what they write, almost routinely, and certainly on a regular basis. Then there are quotations by chairmen of publicly quoted companies and, finally, quotations from numerous other sources, including novels or statements made by people famous in many other walks of life.

As a further item of background information, I am including here a short account of some career aspects of a few of the superstar gurus. Their expertise covers growth and value investing, but some of the most incisive comments assuredly come from the contrarians. By reminding us to constantly be cynical observers of events, especially when bull markets reach unsustainable extremes, they provide timely cautions that can help us keep decision-making firmly grounded in reality rather than in the realms of impossible dreams.

In tandem with collecting quotations by the gurus and experts, you might like to consider building a library of investment books. This does not have to be expensive as some of the best books are now out of print so you may be able to pick them up quite cheaply at library 'sales' of old stock or even at local car boot sales. This is another treasure hunt I greatly enjoy. Some of my most exciting finds have cost pennies rather than pounds and nothing compares with the pleasure you can derive from reading a first-hand account on some investment topic that interests you. A little book I found in an Oxfam shop, called *Money*, included this comment by Kevin Lynch in *What Time is This Place?* His observation seemed to encapsulate why we all need successful investments;

'Our most important responsibility to the future is ... to attend to it.'

When I prepared the *Treasury* layout, I did not at first realise that listing the guru quotations in alphabetical order would put Warren Buffett's contributions at the head of almost every theme. This is entirely proper however, since he is undoubtedly a phenomenal colossus towering over a firmament of brilliant super-investors.

WARREN BUFFETT

In the arcane world of investment giants, Warren Buffett scoops all the accolades. Justifiably, he is a venerated figure, building a business empire centred on his investment company, Berkshire Hathaway. He has turned an initial investment of about $100 in the 1950s into a personal fortune worth, on conservative estimates in mid-1999, about $18 billion. This figure will clearly fluctuate with market valuations as it is tied up in Berkshire Hathaway, but he is the second wealthiest man in the world, after Bill Gates, chairman and co-founder of Microsoft.

Many informed commentators remark on his excellent good humour and love of everything he does related to the businesses he owns or plans to own. He himself emphasises how critical it is to determine the intrinsic value of a business and then pay only a fair or bargain price to become a part-owner in it. He abhors investing in businesses he does not understand or that lie outside his 'circle of competence'. He is a master at calculating risk. This discipline has given him his winning edge. Moreover, he insists that twelve investment decisions in his forty-year career have made all the difference to his results.

Can the average investor benefit from Warren Buffett's expertise? Almost everyone has some professional or personal involvement with a sector of the economy or an industry that endows him or her with a superior knowledge over others. Indeed, the notion of focusing on just a few holdings fits excellently with the financial limitations most private investors face. Although Berkshire Hathaway is now a vast company, worth billions, for many years around seventy-five per cent of its common stock holdings were invested in only five different securities.

One of Warren Buffett's driving ambitions is to buy great businesses when they are going through a temporary setback or when the market itself declines, thereby creating bargains in companies with outstanding franchises. Although he pays scant attention to stock market direction, the level of interest rates, the state of the economy and other global issues, his success is embedded in the fortunes of the great American economy. Through forty years, American industry and innovation has led the world. Yet, faithful to his philosophy of investing within his circle of competence, it is a sobering thought that his success has completely side-stepped America's superb high technology sector: it lies primarily with insurance, renowned consumer brands and newspaper companies. Beyond the ambit of his investments, there extends an impressive array of American world-leading companies in numerous sectors that he has chosen to ignore.

One of the most encouraging aspects of Warren Buffett's success is that he freely acknowledges the debt he owes to his teacher and mentor, Benjamin Graham. Yet he in turn has enriched millions of investors, not only those who own shares in Berkshire Hathaway, but through his annual reports. These are avidly collected by devoted disciples because they are replete with Warren Buffett's home-spun insights into investment wisdom. They have been collected into a volume and published under the title, *The Essays of Warren Buffett: Lessons for Corporate America*.

DR MARC FABER

Dr Faber is one of the outstanding financial and investment personalities in the field today. As a Hong Kong-based investment adviser, he gained his reputation as a controversial doomster with a penchant for deep research into the important key issues of the day. His sweeping intellect scans the financial markets and global economies to discover and analyse the over-arching mega-trends. For long-term investors, these are the themes that demand the closest attention.

He takes a somewhat discursive stand on major topics, interpreting the future from well-researched historical precedents. During the 1990s, with a prolonged bull market running, he has acquired some dubious titles, 'The Prince of Pessimism' or 'The Godfather of Gloom'. In essence, he is a contrarian to the core, always keen to steer the readers of his regular newsletter, 'The Gloom, Boom and Doom Report', away from the obvious excess crowd reactions so they can avoid the pitfalls inherent in that stance. Accordingly, some of his most profound remarks concern the ever-present tendency of investors to become wildly over-enthusiastic about their investment prospects when a strong dose of realism would definitely serve them better. A highly readable account of Marc Faber's investment philosophy appears in Nury Vittachi's book, *Riding the Millennial Storm*.

PETER LYNCH

Peter Lynch is one of my favourite gurus. He was spectacularly successful as manager of the gigantic Fidelity Magellan Fund; an investment of $1,000 in 1977 into Magellan grew to almost $19,000 by his retirement in 1990. Under his stewardship, this flagship company, the most famous of the large-scale mutual funds that invest for capital growth rather than dividends, became a household name due to this amazing performance.

Like Warren Buffet, Peter Lynch is another exceptional value investor. He bought major stakes in companies that had temporarily fallen out of favour. At the time of his purchases, they were selling less, making lower profits than previously, and had often run up staggering debts. He spent hours of detailed research poring over annual reports, analysing the fundamentals and ferreting out the important figures within the publicly available information. Having satisfied himself that the chosen companies would not fail, thereby wiping out his total investment, he was ready to take large bets. His method illustrates the compelling maxim, 'Knowledge is power'.

With this routine, two of his greatest successes were Ford and Chrysler, the two giant motor companies. He bought them as recovery situations in the early 1980s because they were grossly undervalued by the market, due to falling sales, unpopular models and mounting debts. There was much discussion by commentators on whether Chrysler would survive or go bankrupt. Having bought his stakes for Magellan, he sat and waited for the two car giants to recover their profitability. As the market began to recognise the recovery stories, other investors bought shares, giving him his fantastic returns.

Peter Lynch is convinced that amateur investors have unique advantages over the professionals. In fact, he insists his success at Magellan was due to his ability to 'think like an amateur'. 'Which,' he asked, 'would you rather back—a company that is a big fish in a small pond, or one that is a small fish in a big pond?' The Magellan answer is to look for companies that are about to become the biggest fish in the biggest pond. Peter Lynch has ideas about the big fish/big pond world view that are of interest to investors. According to him, a fund with billions of dollars to invest is like a supertanker: it is not turned around easily and smaller, more nimble, funds can speed by it if they happen to chance upon one or two choice investment opportunities. In this analogy, private investors can be nimble while professional funds are slothful supertankers.

In the early months of 1999, the travails of supertanker funds were thoroughly aired by Warren Buffett when he repeatedly complained about the difficulty of investing Berkshire Hathaway's $15 billion cash war chest at a time when outstanding bargains had all but disappeared. He described this famine as, 'A fat wallet is the enemy of superior investment returns.'

Peter Lynch thinks the supertankers' dilemma creates a magnificent opening for amateurs. He insists everyone can go hunting investments with an elephant gun and still bag some impressive prizes. In America, the Standard & Poor's 500 index comprised companies worth $11,000 billion by mid-1999. When you add in the 500 biggest companies elsewhere in the world, the total value was $18,000 billion. Even assuming these values shrink if the great 1990s global bull market falters, Peter Lynch concludes there are more than enough opportunities to score handsome gains.

Investors wanting to delve more deeply into his outstandingly successful investment philosophy can read his two best-selling investment books, *One Up on Wall Street*, and the sequel, *Beating the Street*, both of which are packed with techniques and analysis invaluable to private investors.

WILLIAM O'NEIL

William O'Neil has one of the most common-sense attitudes I have yet encountered on running a successful portfolio. Among the constellation of superstar gurus, he ranks very highly with me, because I am in tune with his general philosophy and approach. He is a growth investor par excellence, with a formidable track record of success. His investment book has a blunt, no nonsense title, *How to Make Money in Stocks*. It may sound like hubris, but it is reassuring for investors. You know, right away, that he is going to share with his readers all the depth of his research and years of experience, neatly packaged under his own special formula, his CAN SLIM recipe for stock-picking success.

Although he is a growth investor utilising key fundamental information as a basis for investing, he is also a chartist, or technical analyst. He studies charts of share prices and the main market indices when he is weighing up share prospects or market direction. His speciality is applying the CAN SLIM formula to the host of small growth companies available for investors in America, but I know from my own study of his method that his techniques travel quite comfortably across the Atlantic. Although he is undoubtedly a super-successful investor, I believe the range of his expertise is easily within the competence of most small investors, especially if they are keen to put in the necessary effort.

JIM ROGERS

Jim Rogers came from such a small Southern town, his telephone number was just 5. Yet he became another great Wall Street legend, making his fortune during the 1970s by managing the Quantum Fund with George Soros. At the age of thirty-seven he retired to spend his time investing his own funds while doing a host of different things. One of these was to become a finance professor at Columbia University. Never short of daring, he combined one of his great passions, motorcycling, with curiosity about the world's developing countries. Early in the 1990s he set a world record for land travel, covering over sixty-five thousand miles while he explored the global economy and the countries he visited en route. He wrote an absorbing account of his trip in *Investment Biker*.

Among his great attributes is his notorious attitude to the crowd. Jim Rogers is a quintessential contrarian. He realised that the semi-moribund Austrian market could be revived and made a fortune from this one insight.

JIM SLATER

Jim Slater, the most famous UK private investor, is renowned on several fronts associated with investment. As a chartered accountant he rose to prominence during the 1960s and was, for ten years (1964 to 1974), chairman of the legendary financial conglomerate, Slater Walker Securities. At its height, Slater Walker Securities was one of the fifty largest UK companies, capitalised at over £200 million. When the company fell into decline during the turbulent 1970s era, he described himself with disarming honesty as a 'minus millionaire'. I strongly believe that the characteristics that differentiate investment winners from losers is their resilience and determination. They are not afraid to confront the traumatic setbacks. How they strive to turn a disaster into a triumph becomes the stuff of legend. Jim Slater's story has all the hallmarks of this impressive journey.

He has written four excellent investment books intended primarily for small private investors to improve their skills. He has also devised a splendid reference manual, *Really Essential Financial Statistics*, (*Company Refs*), published by Hemmington Scott, which has become an indispensable database for professionals and amateurs. *Company Refs* is updated monthly and is available on subscription, but can now also be accessed on the internet at http://www.hemscott.com.

As the most successful UK private investor, he is a brilliant role model for us to follow. The first of his investment books, *The Zulu Principle*, covers in great detail his personal stock-picking system which is especially tailored for unearthing small growth companies at an early stage in their development. His method is also mirrored to some extent in *Company Refs*, where the excellent layout separates essential growth statistics from value so that investors can quickly and more easily focus on whether they want to follow growth or undervalued candidates.

GEORGE SOROS

The reputation of George Soros became indelibly fixed as the man who broke the Bank of England when he famously bet against Britain's remaining in the European Exchange Rate Mechanism during September 1992. Although he was known for over twenty years as one of the shrewdest operators on Wall Street, his elevation to superstar status was founded on the knowledge that his funds made around $1 billion on 'Black Wednesday', when the British government was forced to devalue sterling. In consequence, he became that rarest of investment gurus – a savant with such mystique that his actions alone can move markets around the world.

Interestingly, he moved to America in 1956, around the time when Warren Buffett first began his investment career. After more than forty years of investment expertise, both Soros and Buffett have become legends in their lifetimes for their successful exploits in the markets, but their philosophies could not be more different. Buffett epitomises the cautious long-term investor, while Soros is the quintessential short-term speculator, distinguished by his specialisation in currency and bond markets.

In New York he oversees Soros Fund Management, which sets the investment strategy for the unquoted flagship hedge fund Quantum Group. Unlike most traditional funds, hedge funds are less closely regulated by outsiders or even by internal policy. They are free to use complex speculative trading strategies to maximise the returns they make for the high net-worth individuals who place their funds at the managers' disposal. A standard routine is to use leveraged funds. This is money borrowed against the value of the assets. They also adopt hedging strategies, the most common of which is to sell short (selling a security that is not owned by the fund in the hope that later, when it has to be delivered to the owner, it can be bought back at a lower price). Selling short was the technique used before 'Black Wednesday' when George Soros began selling sterling he did not own. Other Wall Street gurus acknowledge his greatest trait as a willingness to reverse his position instantaneously as soon as he recognises he has made a mistake.

During the 1970s George Soros and his then partner, Jim Rogers, gained a reputation for shorting some stocks that were firm favourites of established fund managers, including Disney and Polaroid. He described as 'the killing of a lifetime' his speculation against the yen in 1985 at the time when the Plaza Accord generated an enormous overvaluation of the yen. Aggressive speculation creates extremes in both winners and losers. Soros freely admits he lost money on currencies in the four years before the Plaza Accord and most famously, Quantum Fund was estimated to have lost around $800 million in the 1987 Wall Street crash. However, the run-up to that October collapse had been so immense, the fund was still able to record investment returns of 14 per cent for the full year. Interestingly, during 1987 he was warning that the Japanese market was so wildly overpriced, a crash there was almost inevitable. Although he did not foresee the October collapse would centre on Wall Street, he was absolutely right about the overvaluation in Tokyo. The rampant Japanese bull market quickly righted itself after the shock waves of October 1987 had subsided, but the peak was reached two years later. Beginning in December 1989, the catastrophe that ultimately brought down Japanese equity prices was far more insidious than an outright crash: it was a decade-long slump which mired the country in a still on-going period of intractable depression.

With his monumental profits from speculation, George Soros has gradually withdrawn from daily involvement in the funds, and has established foundations in Eastern Europe, where he spends more of his time. This is ample evidence that acquiring billions is not a problem if you are interested in people and in philanthropy.

SIR JOHN TEMPLETON

John Templeton spent over forty years as one of the world's most famous and successful fund managers. He was an early pioneer of global investing and his expertise spanned many decades, from the 1930s to the 1980s. Today his associates still travel the world searching for bargains using the value-investing routines that he instilled. They are looking for stocks that most investors have ignored, which are selling at a fraction of their intrinsic value. Focusing on these bargains has produced tremendous annual growth rates for the Templeton funds.

Like other unbelievably successful investors, he insists that following the few basic investment principles that underpin his methods can enable others to emulate his success. His story is told in *Global Investing: The Templeton Way*, as related by Norman Berryessa and Eric Kirzner.

BILL WILLIAMS

I doubt if many UK investors will have heard of Bill Williams, although he has a great following among futures traders in America, as many of them consider him to be among the most brilliant educators in the field. This expertise justifies his ranking here as a guru of note. He has over forty years' experience as both a successful trader and a seasoned trainer. I first came across Bill Williams in 1998, by reading his book, *Trading Chaos*, published by John Wiley. His pioneering application of chaos theory puts a twenty-first century gloss on technical analysis, and although few gurus use it, I am a great fan both of technical analysis and the power of chaos theory as applied to financial markets.

Bill Williams has some truly innovative ideas about investment practice and I learned a huge amount from reading *Trading Chaos*. Later, I read the follow-up volume, *New Trading Dimensions*. I am as far removed from a speculative trader as it is possible to be, but I still found a wealth of investment knowledge here in these two books ready and available for eager readers to absorb. In consequence, some of his most profound quotes are featured in the *Treasury*.

1 Market Wisdom

••••••••••••••••••••••••••••••

Investment is a niche area of human endeavour that encompasses some of the most raw emotions people can experience. Financial markets are the theatre on which these emotions are nakedly displayed: hope, fear, greed, exultation and despair. Unexpected thrills and spills are so inherent in the chase for wealth that over the past few decades the subject of investment has developed its own jargon-ridden language, arcane customs and lexicon of beliefs. The basis of this first theme, therefore, is to tap into a rich stream of sayings that have become part of the very culture of investing. Many of the most well-rehearsed sayings have acquired the respectability of axioms. They are venerated in the markets by their worldliness and time-honoured usage. Although events are continually changing and the future hard to predict for most market practitioners, the relevance of these sayings seems incredibly enduring.

Clearly, such sayings form a natural starting point in any treasury of investment wisdom, but additionally, I have included a short collection of my father's most favoured investment expressions: they have served me well over the years. As he was the first proper armchair investor I ever knew, his sayings were foremost in my thoughts during my earliest investment experiences.

Finally, in this first theme, there is a range of sayings by fund managers. Collectively, these are the experts we entrust with our savings, hoping they will employ successful investment strategies to enhance our future nest eggs.

Although I always pay close attention to what the professionals have to say, I still maintain the priority task for small private investors is to become their own financial advisers. When you hand your affairs over to a financial expert, you lose control. Sadly, financial scandals are far too prevalent for comfort; if you get caught up in one such disaster, you may find you have unwittingly become an expert while sorting it out. It would clearly be better to acquire this knowledge before a financial morass wreaks havoc with your long-term investment plans.

It makes good sense to listen to the experts but equally, everyone should try to take their own advice and assume the exciting responsibility of making their own money grow. You have to become your own financial adviser to fully experience the pleasure it brings when your hard-fought efforts succeed. Logically, no one will take as much care over your finances as you yourself. Statistics show that the vast majority of professionals do not match the benchmark indices against which they measure their performance. Yet, despite this failing, we can still gain valuable insights from what they say.

Axioms
....

Bull markets climb a wall of worry.

What goes up must come down.

The trend is your friend.

Sell in May and go away.

As January goes, so goes the remainder of the year.

Buy on the rumour, sell on the news.

Buy low and sell high.

Never catch falling knives.

Nothing new ever occurs in the markets.

No one rings a bell when the market peaks.

Hasty climbers can have sudden falls.

By the time the smoke has lifted, the train has left the station.

The market is never wrong.

Failure teaches success.

When Wall Street sneezes, London catches cold.

Look for the opportunities thrown up when the tides of despondency reach a flood.

The definition of a long-term investment is a short-term investment that went wrong.

One of the most misleading stock market saws is the one that says in order to make money you have to go against the crowd. That only starts to make sense if you add the qualifier '... go against the crowd and be right.'
Philip Ryland, Investors Chronicle

The main lesson for investors is an old adage: question anything that promises regular returns higher than those available on the stock market. The promise of a 51 per cent return should pull anyone's head out of the sand.
Paul Ham, The Sunday Times, *on the wind-up of OFC (the Ostrich Farming Corporation) in March 1996*

My Father's Favourite Sayings

Don't be greedy. Leave something for the next investor.

Don't rely on a crystal ball for stock-picking.
It may be cracked.

You make your own luck.

Don't worry about things you can't change, worry about things you can change.

Why use your own money to buy a house when you can use someone else's?

Fund Managers' Sayings

Most managers have very little incentive to make the intelligent-but-with-some-chance-of-looking-like-an-idiot decision.
Warren Buffett

It will not be a matter of which sector will perform when the economy improves but the nature of the company.
John Alexander, investment manager, Smaller Companies unit trust, Henderson Touche Remnant

You can't expect a fund manager to outperform in every period you take. I'd be happy if he outperforms in 14 or 15 out of 20 periods.
Clive Boothman, chairman of Autif, the UK's unit trusts trade body

By definition, the FTSE 100 is a winners' index. Like the Premier League, the worst teams keep getting rooted out, and you have to be good to stay in the top tier.
Robert Buckland, UK equity strategist at stockbroker, NatWest

I do not subscribe to the view that, because a company doesn't have earnings, it doesn't have value.
Paul Cook, a US-based fund manager for Framlington's new unit trust, The NetNet Unit Trust, spring 1999

If you are going to put a lump sum into the market every year, the autumn is generally the best time to do it.
Mark Dampier, Hargreaves Lansdown, independent financial advisers

There is a lot of show biz in active fund management. Investors pay a lot for a promise that can only be delivered by chance.
Pattie Dunn, chairman of Barclays Global Investors, managing £370 billion, the world's largest institutional fund manager

Sector rotation always creates tugs of war between the bulls and the bears.
Ben Funnel, strategist for Morgan Stanley Dean Witter

It is not the economic cycle that is controlling the stock market, it's the mood cycle and the mood is to buy stocks.
Alfred Goldman, chief market strategist at G. Edwards in St Louis

I don't think the level of the stock market, or the fact that savings appear to be declining, is indicative of the future of the retirement savings market.
Maurice Greenberg, chairman of American International Group

If an investor can afford to take full stock market risk, then it is difficult to say he shouldn't buy a tracker versus a generalist fund.
Peter Jeffreys, managing director of Standard & Poor's Fund Research

I am a generalist, with a background in numeracy and economics, and generalists tend to make good fund managers.
Malcolm 'Max' King, fund manager with J.O. Hambros & Partners

My attitude is towards a core of solid growth companies, and the riskier stocks should be the icing on the cake.
Malcolm 'Max' King, fund manager with J.O. Hambros & Partners

The market is always right.
Paddy Linaker of M & G Group

As long as the year-on-year trend is for the rate of earnings growth to fall, it's not going to be a good idea to buy lesser quality companies.
A. Marshall Acuff Jr., portfolio strategist at Smith Barney

We try and find companies that have a management team in place. When small companies fail it is usually because one man has tried to take on too much.
John McClure, investment manager, Guinness Flight

What I try to look for is a trigger, like a management change, a move up to a main market listing, or if a company is making a significant acquisition.
John McClure, investment manager, Guinness Flight

The figures confirm our belief that the stock market is the best place for long-term savings.
Ian Millward, Chase de Vere, independent financial adviser

Long term, in the smaller company sector you may be able to identify what will become tomorrow's star performer.
Richard Peirson, head of UK equities at Framlington

The nightmare scenario for anyone in the industry is that there will be nowhere to hide in terms of poor products or poor performance.
Stephen Richardson, managing director of Save & Prosper

The stock market remains overpopulated with relatively immature biopharma companies which have shown themselves to be adept at raising money and exceptionally talented at consuming it.
Brian Ashford-Russell, director and manager of Henderson Technology

It's a bizarre commentary on the inertness of bank customers that Barclays could be run without a chief executive for nine months without it damaging the business.
Simon Samuels, banking analyst at Salomon Smith Barney

Don't worry about markets; focus on companies and keep an eagle eye on currencies.
Nils Taube, chief executive for J. Rothschild, equity holdings

Companies are commenting on how profitable they are, which means they are hitting peak margins.
Paul Walton, UK strategist at Goldman Sachs

History belongs to the bulls.
Christopher Walker, director at Hill Samuel, fund manager

We see no reason to change our mind because the market always returns to 'fair value', based on the relative value of bonds and their attractiveness to investors.
Spokesman for Warburg Dillon Read

The US investor does not see dividend income as a big deal although in the UK it is different.
Christopher Clarke, managing director of Witan Investment Trust

I was always interested in investing, although my father believed that anything to do with the stock market was a very idle way of making a living.
Christopher Clarke, managing director of Witan Investment Trust

The Fed is happy to use wealth destruction caused by falling equities to take the froth out of inflation.
Chris Godding, joint fund manager of SocGen's Technology Fund

You didn't have to be a genius to buy Microsoft. It is regarded as a US stock but in reality it is global.
Guy Manson, investment director of Sarasin Investment Management

Even now there is more money in pubs and breweries within the FTSE 100 than any IT stock.
Guy Manson, investment director of Sarasin Investment Management

The FTSE 100 index is a collection of yesterday's success stories. It says nothing about tomorrow.
Guy Manson, investment director of Sarasin Investment Management

2 The Market

....

The market is clearly a central theme for both amateur and professional investors. So much has been written that this theme can comfortably stand alone. Tony Jackson, in the *Financial Times*, made this succinct remark, 'It is worth recalling what the stock market is there for. It's primary purpose is to channel savings to companies that can put them to better use than the savers can themselves'.

Obviously, people who invest directly in company shares might want to know broadly what the financial markets are doing. Less obviously, perhaps, is why it should interest the general public. Yet even if you have savings, insurance policies, pensions or investments in unit or investment trusts, the way markets behave may be equally crucial to the success of your financial plans.

Of course, the market is unpredictable but that does not mean it is a waste of time to follow it. Learning about the markets is time well spent. I reason that if I don't know where the market has been, I cannot possibly judge where it is going. Many experts and gurus suggest it is useless to assess where the market is heading, but for ordinary mortals insights here can be immensely helpful, especially if they indicate timely actions.

To the uninitiated, market behaviour often looks contrary and extreme, catching the headlines at the time of maximum euphoria or anxiety. It seems totally perverse that markets fall on good news. Investors hope for good news, but are perplexed to see when it comes that the market often falls. On the other hand, if bad news is expected and the news is good, the market will rejoice. Even when you expect the unexpected the market can still surprise you. This perversity becomes understandable when you realise the stock market is a forward indicator, discounting the future. It reflects the likely outlook nine to twelve months ahead. This means the market may rise or fall long before the headline-grabbing event.

I find that markets constantly throw up useful clues when I am tuned in to receive them. By watching the market action you avoid the hugely expensive folly of buying shares at a peak. You are in better control of events when you become more aware of what makes the market move because in general, a drifting market is a poor environment for making profits.

Naturally, there are caveats. We should treat the market with respect, or it may bring us down to earth with a bump. Very little is glaringly obvious in the stock market but above all else, it hates uncertainty.

Professional investors dominate the market so huge moves occur when they act in concert. Herd behaviour is noticeable as they hug the mainstream and it may need a major shift in sentiment to change the market's view of a particular happening or company share.

The facts are on your side to ensure you can profit from your newly-gained knowledge about market behaviour because, historically, in the last eighty years shares rose more consistently than they fell. I first began investing because I thought the money was sitting in the market: to get myself out of debt, all I needed was a reliable method to take out my share of it. Nine years on, I still believe this to be the case, but now I am no longer in debt. What the gurus and experts say about the markets reveals interesting angles on how you might exploit this fascinating arena of human endeavour for yourself.

As far as I am concerned, the stock market doesn't exist. It is only there as a reference to see if anybody is offering to do anything foolish.
Warren Buffett

Don't think about what the market's going to do; you have absolutely no control over that. Think about what you're going to do if it gets there.
William Eckhardt, futures trader

Markets are more synchronised than ever.
Dr Marc Faber, editor of 'The Gloom, Boom and Doom Report'

Markets are no different to empires. They expand, rise in value, become over-extended, and eventually collapse.
Dr Marc Faber, editor of 'The Gloom, Boom & Doom Report'

In the short run the stock market is a voting machine: in the long run, it's a weighing machine.
Benjamin Graham

The stock market demands conviction; it victimises the unconvinced.
One Up on Wall Street, *Peter Lynch*

It seems to me to be most important not to be upset out of one's permanent holdings by being too attentive to market movements. Unless one believes the market movement to be well founded, taking a long view, I should like in a case where I felt real confidence, to ignore it.

John Maynard Keynes. Letter to fellow directors of Provincial Insurance Company, August 1934

Yet it is one of the great paradoxes of the stock market that what seems too high usually goes higher and what seems too low usually goes lower.

William O'Neil

It doesn't matter what you think the market will do. All that matters is what the market actually does do.

William O'Neil

Investors' personal opinions are generally wrong; markets seldom are.

William O'Neil

Personal feelings and opinions are far less accurate than markets.

William O'Neil

If the market keeps going the way it shouldn't go, especially if it is a hysterical blowoff, then you know an opportunity will present itself.

Jim Rogers

Permit me to share with you … [why] I love trading the markets. It is the last bastion of free enterprise where you are rewarded generously for doing the easy, appropriate thing. You win or lose purely on your own decisions.

New Trading Dimensions, Bill Williams

Your beliefs about the market create your reality about
the market.
New Trading Dimensions, *Bill Williams*

You should understand that no individual or company
is large enough, strong enough, or smart enough to
control the markets.
New Trading Dimensions, *Bill Williams*

QUESTION Jack Schwager:
What are the major misconceptions people have about the
stock market?
ANSWER Richard Driehaus:
They tend to confuse short-term volatility with long-term
risk. The longer the term, the lower the risk of holding
equities.
Taken from 'The New Market Wizards', Jack D. Schwager

The markets are the same now as they were five to ten
years ago because they keep changing – just like they
did then.
Ed Seykota, futures trader

You will never find the exact bottom of the market. The
aim is to buy when the index is relatively low.
Jim Slater, Analyst, September 1990

The direct relationship between interest rates and
stock markets is notorious.
John Train, chairman of Montrose Advisers

But markets are not that simple. Rising prices usually
fuel more buying.
John Train

To succeed you must use the clues market action provides.
Stan Weinstein, publisher of The Professional Tape Reader

The desire to regard bad news as good news is a common,
and sometimes hilarious, symptom of market mania. Is
the market going up? 'Get in quick!' Is the market going
down? 'It's a buying opportunity!'
Riding the Millennial Storm, *Nury Vittachi*

The market tends to be the best judge of what is going to
happen and the best place to invest your money.
Gordon Maw, Virgin Direct

You've got to have the ability to step back from the
emotional element of what's happening in the market and
say, 'What does this company represent? What does it do?
Is the market getting it wrong?'
Stephen Peak, senior European fund manager at Henderson Touche Remnant

The market can afford to pay more for earnings when
interest rates are coming down.
Satya Pradhuman, manager of US quantitative analysis at Merrill Lynch

As far as the US is concerned, most people believe that
every time we get to a magic round number the market
draws a breath before it moves to a higher level.
*David Butler, head of sales at Teather & Greenwood, March 1999 when the
Dow first fleetingly breached 10,000*

I have noticed that everyone who has ever told me that
the markets are efficient is poor.
Larry Hite, Mint Investment Management Company

Expectations do have a way of running too high, and the
market does have a way of correcting those expectations.
*Edward C. Johnson, chairman at Fidelity Investments, America's largest fund
management group*

It's the unexpected that does the market in.
Joe Battipaglia, chief investment strategist at Gruntal & Co

When markets and investors get emotional, it creates
fantastic buying opportunities, because there's no
discrimination between what should go down and
what does go down.
*Yves Tack, head of international equity trading at Banque Nationale de Paris
in London*

If one market is weak, out of safety the other markets
will react and so will fund managers who are running
international books.
Justin Urquhart Stewart, a director of Barclays stockbrokers

This correction isn't over. Markets don't go straight
down. They go down hard, get oversold, rally, then
go down again.
Byron Wein, market strategist at Morgan Stanley

The first move of being defensive is to diversify. As
markets become more and more global that becomes
increasingly difficult.
Ian Beauchamp, director and chief economist at Hambros Fund Management

The UK stock market is curiously skewed. Four sectors—
banks, telecommunications services, pharmaceuticals and
oil and gas—account for 46 per cent of the FTSE All-Share
and 56 per cent of the FTSE 100 index (though, strangely,
only 4 per cent of the FTSE 250).
Barry Riley, Financial Times

What's the market gonna do, sir?
Fluctuate, my boy, just fluctuate.
*Alleged conversation between J. Pierpont Morgan, the banker, and an
elevator boy in 1929*

A total of 50% of the world's market capitalisation is in the US, so investors should have some exposure to it.
Ian Millward, Chase de Vere, independent financial adviser

When the stock market sneezes the new issues market tends to catch cold.
Lex Column, Financial Times

A curious feature of capital markets is their ability to become irrationally obsessed with a single monthly statistic.
Leader article, Financial Times, *10 June 1996*

This is the first time that I recall expressing a view on stock markets anywhere. But if the pundits in any field seem to be living in a fantasy land one must say so.
Samuel Brittan, 'Economic Viewpoint', Financial Times, *13 May 1999*

The big new opportunity today is to persuade a rapidly ageing and increasingly long lived population that it can buy a cosy old age through the securities market.
Barry Riley, Financial Times

Real time exercises in economic opinion polling [are] the financial markets.
Barry Riley, Financial Times

The faster the economy grows, the less happy is the bond market.
Maggie Urry, 'Weekend Money', Financial Times

Markets hate inflation. It pushes interest rates up, drags down bond prices and has a knock-on effect on equities.
Maggie Urry, 'Weekend Money', Financial Times

The US stock market is a land of giants.
John Authers, Financial Times

Although the market receives an enormous amount of
economic analysis to chew over daily, it is difficult to get
beyond the impact of the latest monthly stats.
'Fund Manager', Investors Chronicle

Sometimes in markets when everything appears confused,
a solution to the way ahead lies at hand if only we can see
it through the murk.
'Fund Manager', Investors Chronicle

The yield at the long end of the US bond market has a
powerful impact on markets everywhere.
'Fund Manager', Investors Chronicle

The American media, bored with non-eventful year 2000
stories, have suddenly discovered Dow 10,000.
Anatole Kaletsky, The Times

The stock market is important, precisely because it is a
leading indicator.
Patrick Tooher and Tom Stevenson, The Independent

The London equity market now has a FTSE information
technology sector. It came into operation today (1 April—
no jokes please).
'Fund Manager', Investors Chronicle

The markets may change, but people don't.
Larry Hite, Mint Investment Management Company

Sometimes market movements seem completely irrational
and have more to do with sentiment than any concrete news.
Karen Zagor, The Times

Stock markets like a situation where the monetary authorities will keep money very easy and interest rates low because the outlook for growth looks so uncertain.
Roger Nightingale, economist

History shows that London and Wall Street both rise consistently in the year preceding an American presidential election.
David Schwartz, editor of The Schwartz Stock Market Handbook

Bond markets have their periods of jitters but as long as the inflation numbers stay reassuringly low there is unlikely to be a major setback.
Quentin Lumsden, Chart Breakout

Stock Exchange, risky, of course with the country in its present anxious state. [1801, but could just as easily be 1939, 1974, 1983 or 1995, or any year in between]. Fortunes easily won, but more easily lost. Unless you're an expert in the game, it's one best left untouched.
Thomas Taylor to Mary Anne, in Mary Anne, Daphne Du Maurier

You can't buck the markets.
Margaret Thatcher

When you send a fool to market, the merchants rejoice.
Leo Rosten

The financial markets are so well developed that it does not matter where you are located to be a global company.
Kevin Lomax, executive chairman of Misys, a leading UK computer software company

3 The Optimistic Surge

Under the theme of optimism I have drawn together the art of buying, including companies buying other companies, plus quotations about bull markets. I personally believe the reason why the market rises more than it falls reflects the long-term increase in economic growth in the industrialised and newly industrialising nations. Since 1918, medical advances and technology have transformed the lives of millions. As the twentieth century progressed, more people than ever before were living into their eighties and enjoying the products of inventions and discoveries which only one hundred years earlier seemed unimaginable: electricity, radio, travel by car and aeroplane, telephone, refrigeration, television, plastics, computers; the list is virtually endless. All these products must be manufactured and are then sold in monumental quantities to enthusiastic consumers so the markets are open-ended for profitable ventures to succeed.

There may be setbacks along the route, but this long-run scenario is not in jeopardy, because inventions with profitable opportunities continue to emerge.

Bull Markets

On several occasions I have found the best tonic for a jaded investment performance is the arrival of a new bull market.

It starts when investors are flush with cash and anticipate fat company profits. It is wonderful news if you have most of your money invested in the market just before it begins a strong rise. The secret of making greater than average profits is to buy ahead of the crowd when the bull market is still relatively young. As William O'Neil writes in *How to Make Money in Stocks*, 'The big money is made in the first two years of a bull market.' If you are not in the market when it suddenly enjoys a big run up you may never regain those lost profits. Timing market moves is a difficult skill to master, which is a strong argument in favour of long-term investing. During a great bull market, a buy and hold investment strategy can reap spectacular rewards. A patient approach can bring five- to ten-fold returns on your initial investment outlay.

When the market mood is bullish, problems are ignored and prices surge ahead on good news. Unfortunately, boom and bust seems to be just an uncomfortable bi-product of the awesome complexity in running modern industrial economies. The truly spectacular booms—that become bubbles—arise through a huge pyramid of cheap, readily available cash, so understanding the volatile rhythms of boom and bust in economic life throws up fantastic investment opportunities for those smart enough to follow the cycles. Even in the last stages of a boom, making good profits is still possible: knowing when to withdraw them intact is the clever trick that separates canny investors from the late arrivals. The gurus are adept at extracting profits from the markets and have plenty of powerful comments on bull markets.

I have to admit that the strength of the recent bull market
in the U.S. has taught me to use the word 'impossible'
more carefully.
Dr Marc Faber, editor of 'The Gloom, Boom & Doom Report'

In a bull market your game is to buy and hold until you
believe that the bull market is near its end. To do this you
must study general conditions and not tips or special
factors affecting individual stocks.
Jesse Livermore

The big money is made in the first two years of a bull
market.
How to Make Money in Stocks, *William O'Neil*

Major bull markets begin when institutional cash is higher
than normal and bull markets usually top out when cash
positions are lower than normal.
William O'Neil

By every traditional measure—low dividends, high price
to earnings ratios, staggering volumes on trades—
a top was near.
Investment Biker, *Jim Rogers*

This has been the biggest bull market in the UK and US
this century, and it is the largest overvaluation.
Tony Dye, chief investment officer at Philips & Drew

The market has been going up for five and a half years—
we've never had such a prolonged bull phase in stock
market history without a major correction. Most
Americans now think this is the norm, but in fact
it's an aberration.
Jim Rogers, 'Weekend Money', The Times, 6 April 1996

International capital flows are notorious for their boom–bust pattern and I cannot believe the present boom will not be followed by bust until history has proved me wrong.
George Soros, speaking at the International Monetary Fund annual conference in Hong Kong, September 1997

The usual bull market successfully weathers a number of tests until it is considered invulnerable, whereupon it is ripe for a bust.
George Soros, quoted in The New Money Masters *by John Train*

There's an old saying that bull markets don't die of old age, it's the Fed that kills them.
Rupert de la Porter, Hill Samuel Asset Management, North American desk

One of the reasons I have been feeling more bullish is that there is so much bearishness around.
Barton M. Biggs

It's hard to stop a bull market, and even with all the reversal days, bearish interest rate trends, lagging secondary stocks and record low dividend yields, the bull market might right itself and go even higher.
Martin Zweig, 'Zweig Forecast', 9 October 1987

Riley's Law of Bull Markets: Rationalisations expand to match the market rises that need to be justified.
Barry Riley, Financial Times

In a great bull market, rational analysis can become an embarrassment. Share prices always go up. You must, say the bulls, invest in America's great growth companies, almost at any price: get in, or at any rate get indexed.
Barry Riley, Financial Times

The focus, arguably, should be on how to make money out of the century's greatest bull market, not to fret about how it will end.
Barry Riley, Financial Times

The resultant collision later this year [1999] between US monetary policy and stampeding stock market bulls will crucially influence the direction of global markets.
John Plender, Financial Times

Bull markets are robust phenomena. It is a healthy sign that so many people are looking for this one to end. Much more dangerous is when the financial pages are complacently optimistic.
Quentin Lumsden, editor of Chart Breakout

Genius is a short memory in a bull market.
The Great Crash, *J. K. Galbraith*

Buying

During a rising market, investor behaviour seems to defy the laws of economics. When prices rise, consumers generally cut back their spending. But in the stock market, precisely the opposite happens: when the market is rising, everyone wants to buy. Yet sometimes a fall in prices is a good buying opportunity. Understanding human psychology can be of great help in unravelling the constant struggle between buyers (optimists) and sellers (pessimists) because useful buying clues are always appearing. The old market adage, 'Buy low and sell high', may simply be a cliché, not a realistic blueprint for action. Most investors realise that to make the really super gains, you have to buy well ahead of the exciting news you are expecting in the shares you follow. We can turn to the gurus here; their insights reveal the key criteria for making shrewd purchasing decisions.

Buy a share of stock as though you were buying
the whole company.
Warren Buffett

We like to buy businesses. We don't like to sell and we
expect the relationship to last a lifetime.
Warren Buffett

It is almost a mathematical impossibility to imagine that,
out of thousands of things for sale on a given day, the
most attractively priced is the one being sold by a
knowledgeable seller.
Warren Buffett, on the dangers of buying shares in flotations

I like buying companies that can be run by monkeys—
because one day they will be.
Peter Lynch

If a stock is down but the fundamentals still look good,
hold on or better still, buy more.
One Up on Wall Street, *Peter Lynch*

The insider has only one reason to buy: to make money.
Peter Lynch, quoted in The New Money Masters *by John Train*

A company will rarely go bust in the face of heavy
insider buying.
Peter Lynch, quoted in The New Money Masters *by John Train*

I have an edge because a lot of people I compete with are not looking for reasons to buy. They are looking for reasons not to buy.

Peter Lynch, quoted in The New Money Masters *by John Train*

The best time to invest is when blood is running in the streets.

Lord William Rees Mogg

Money was flooding the world. Every stock market in the world was at an all-time high. You had all these young guys, three years out of school, making half a million dollars a year. That is not reality. Whenever you see that in a market, you are near a top.

Jim Rogers, on the build-up to the October 1987 crash

I never buy at the bottom and I always sell too soon.

Nathan Rothschild

Clearly it pays to buy into fear when prices are low (and dividend yields are high) instead of buying into greed when share prices are high (and dividend yields are low).

Jim Slater

The best time to invest is when it is extremely difficult to summon up the courage to do so. This is usually when the market is relatively low and the outlook is murky.

Jim Slater, Analyst, September 1990

The best time to buy long-term bonds is when short-term rates are higher than long-term rates …. When the yield is inverted.

George Soros, quoted in The New Money Masters *by John Train*

Buy quality, well managed stocks.

Sir John Templeton

In the stock market the only way to get a bargain is
to buy what most investors are selling.
Sir John Templeton

The time of maximum pessimism is the best time to buy,
and the time of maximum optimism is the best time to sell.
Sir John Templeton

It always pays to buy on a war scare.
John Train, Financial Times

One of the safest times to invest is when the news is awful
and markets are depressed: the Time of Deepest Gloom.
John Train, Financial Times

A good time to move is when the weather has improved
and people are saying: 'Yes, the values are attractive, but
nothing's going to happen for six months.' When you hear
that, look for a buying opportunity.
John Train, Financial Times

When yet another Japanese bank has a scandal, the
chairman commits suicide and the stock stands still, there
are probably few shares left to sell.
John Train, Financial Times

A good indicator is when bad news fails to drive the
market or stock down further or, better still, when it starts
rising against bad news.
John Train, Financial Times

Everybody remembers the dark side of the 1987 crash,
but they tend to forget what a great buying opportunity
it was.
*Graham Hooper, investment director at Chase de Vere,
independent financial advisers*

It is always best to invest in markets at the point of maximum pessimism.

James Mellar, chief executive of Regent Pacific

You have to make a decision to buy or sell or do nothing and often doing nothing can be the right thing.

Stephen Peak, senior European fund manager at Henderson Touche Remnant

Why do income funds systematically outperform? Because they exploit persistent anomalies and are therefore more likely to buy cheaper.

Nick Train, investment fund manager, M&G Group

The credit expansion setting the boom going proceeds by way of the interest rate being 'too low'.

Crises and Cycles, *W. Röpke*

One extraordinary feature of the whole boom was the apparently unlimited willingness of the banks to lend money for railway investment.

The Stock Exchange Story, *Alan Jenkins*

Mergers

A flurry of mergers can be a cyclical event in the market's life. At the height of the bull market, company directors, merchant bankers and brokers become extremely optimistic. Even when companies have debts or are not cash-rich, they may buy acquisitions or make takeovers by offering their highly-priced shares to investors instead of paying them out in cash. Some quotations on company mergers are included as mergers arise when companies make buying decisions about other companies.

When a chief executive officer is encouraged by his advisors to make deals, he responds much as would a teenage boy who is encouraged by his father to have a normal sex life. It's not a push he needs.
Warren Buffett

There have been nine stories for every one actual takeover.
Richard Jeffrey, Charterhouse Group economist

Sir Geoffrey Mulcahy, Kingfisher chief executive, has learnt in France how to make a takeover feel like a merger.
Lex Column, Financial Times

Chief executives seem no more able to resist their biological urge to merge than dogs can resist chasing rabbits.
Philip Coggan, 'Weekend Money', Financial Times

The benefits of many mergers have been lost during the integration phase.
Robert Corzine, Financial Times

When it comes to mergers, hope triumphs over experience.
Irwin Stelzer, The Sunday Times

4 The Pessimistic Urge

Interestingly, more topics are grouped under the theme of pessimism than optimism, because when investors take fright, their fear of the unknown becomes an over-riding force for action. So, in addition to the obvious elements of selling and quotations on bear markets, there are comments on volatility, crashes, crises and crowds. What links them all when most investors and speculators are pessimistic is an irrepressible urge to sell.

The psychological pendulum is as difficult to stop on the downswing as on the upswing, but the market often begins to rise when the general mood in the country is exceptionally gloomy and brave investors increasingly think ahead to better times. The gurus and experts have definite views on market pessimism, so what they say about bear markets, selling decisions, crashes, crowds and volatility is food for thought for investors keen to understand crowd behaviour when pessimism is rampant.

Bear Markets

Sadly, it seems that every economic boom holds the seeds of a recession that will surely follow it. As one of the Federal Reserve's most distinguished chairman said in the 1960s, the job of a central bank is 'to take away the punchbowl just when the party is getting merry'. The price paid for an economic boom is recession—or worse—and in the market, boom can turn amazingly quickly to gloom. Ironically, good news for the economy is often bad news for financial markets.

A popular saying is, 'No one rings a bell when the market peaks.' Yet there are many warning signs to look for. Bull markets usually end when investors face imminent prospects of tighter money and rising interest rates. Universal optimism during the last phases of the upswing occurs as all the bears finally relent and become late converts to the bull market.

Buying shares at the top of the market is foolhardy. If you pay high prices for your shares, your returns may be abysmally low. So how do you know when the market is reaching a top? There is generally so much optimism around at a market top, it is easy to get carried away in a strongly rising market; but if you do this, you may find your gains get carried away when you are left fully invested in the downturn. Therefore, ask yourself, 'When everyone is a buyer, who is left to buy?' Once everyone is enthusiastic about market prospects, the good news has probably all been discounted.

———————————

Overall, Berkshire and its long-term shareholders benefit from a sinking stock market. When the market plummets, neither panic nor mourn.

Warren Buffett, welcoming the 40,000 new shareholders to Berkshire Hathaway, the holding company he leads, who bought shares in the summer of 1996 when the company made an offering of lower-priced B shares

At the start of a bear market, nobody knows it is a bear market—they just think it is a correction.
Dr Marc Faber

A stock market decline is a great opportunity to pick up bargains left behind by investors who are fleeing the storm in panic.
Peter Lynch

Remember that downturns do not last forever, particularly since politicians discovered the antidote—inflation.
John Train, Financial Times

It's always bullish for the major trend that corporate insiders are selling relatively little stock. When most bear markets start, they are selling quite heavily.
Stan Weinstein, Professional Tape Reader, August 1987

BEAR: An endangered species on Wall Street.
Suzanne McGee, Wall Street Journal

But the Catch-22 with these cycles is that since they are of indeterminate scale and duration by the time you know for sure that you are in a bull or a bear phase it is often nearly over.
Quentin Lumsden, Chart Breakout

Selling

Guru investors are clearly in a league apart, but for most investors, knowing when to sell can be critical to success. This decision becomes a major problem if you do not have a well-defined selling system which eliminates the temptation of holding on to loss situations.

The dilemma of selling is reduced to a minimum for long-term investors, but if you are fond of buying small growth companies with exciting potentials, a disciplined selling routine is indispensable.

The importance of selling can be judged from the numbers of excellent quotations from gurus, confirming my suspicion that a skilled approach to selling is an essential element of portfolio management.

I sold stocks that were rising and that is one reason why I have held on to my fortune.
Bernard Baruch, American financier and statesman

The decision to sell the company's holding in McDonald's was a very big mistake. Overall, you would have been better off last year if I had regularly snuck off to the movies during market hours.
Warren Buffett, annual report 1999, revealing the company's failure to match the gain in the broader stock market, a very rare event

When the ship starts to sink, don't pray. Jump.
The Zurich Axioms, *Max Gunther*

If you are susceptible to selling everything in a panic, you ought to avoid stocks.
Peter Lynch

Only a fool holds out for the top dollar.
Joseph Kennedy, father of President Jack Kennedy, who made a fortune selling shares short in the 1929 Wall Street crash

To be a successful investor, it pays to be slow to sell.
Peter Lynch

Selling when a stock rises is a deluded strategy. It is like pulling out the flowers in the garden and watering the weeds.
Peter Lynch

If you buy a stock because you hope something will happen, and it doesn't happen, sell the stock.
Peter Lynch

Sell a stock because the company's fundamentals deteriorate, not because the sky is falling.
Peter Lynch

If you sell in desperation, you always sell cheap.
Peter Lynch

If the price of a share you are holding sinks like a stone, don't hope, sell.
William O'Neil

Sell down to the sleeping point. The sleeping point varies, depending on your risk tolerance; it may mean one-third, one-half or all of a position.
Harold L. Rosenthal

When all the news is perfect and cheerful tidings fail to lift the stock further, beware!
John Train, Financial Times

You never know what is enough until you know it is more than enough.
Barton Biggs, head of global strategy at Morgan Stanley Dean Witter

Frequently a ruthless investor who sells swiftly will lose less money than those who loyally hold on.
Investors Chronicle

The way to make money on the Exchange is to sell too soon.
Nathan Rothschild

We tend only to sell companies for strategic reasons—if
they make an acquisition or a rights issue we don't agree
with. We sell for those reasons as opposed to selling on the
basis of the price action.
John McClure, investment manager, Guinness Flight

The Dow Jones Industrial Average has just rocketed from
10,000 to 11,000 within a month, posing the question of
whether the US stock market has turned into nothing
more than a giant Ponzi scheme that will collapse when
people want to reclaim their money.
Barry Riley, Financial Times

The art of investment is knowing when to sell.
Investors Chronicle

It's usually better to sell within 10 per cent of the top when
a stock is on its way down, than to sell too early.
Investors Chronicle

Most master investors maintain strict disciplines which
ensure they keep detached and are prepared to sell
holdings.
Investors Chronicle

Sell your cleverness and buy bewilderment.
Jalal Ud-Din Rumi, Persian mystical poet (1207–73)

Volatility

Volatility in share prices, with enormous gyrations,
increases at market peaks and troughs. Evidence for

heightened volatility is therefore a useful signal of an imminent turning point. Volatility spells danger for investors because the buyers and sellers are both dithering. It exposes investor confusion on the next direction of the market, but as John Train notes, 'For the investor who knows what he is doing, volatility creates opportunity.'

Investment markets are volatile beasts and you have to keep an eye on your positions.
Investment Biker, *Jim Rogers*

Short-term volatility (instability) is greatest at turning points and diminishes as the trend is established.
George Soros

For the investor who knows what he is doing, volatility creates opportunity.
John Train, chairman of Montrose Advisors, New York

Asset bubbles threaten not only financial loss and share price volatility but also sharp swings in the economy.
Patrick Tooher and Tom Stevenson, The Independent

Markets have become more volatile. Investors will just have to live with that fact.
Quentin Lumsden, Chart Breakout

What investors have to accept is that these huge returns have a cost in vastly higher risk and volatility.
Quentin Lumsden, Chart Breakout

Crashes
··

Fortunately, stock market crashes are very rare events: so, indeed, are guru comments on them. Yet crashes are so catastrophic and unexpected, that, like air disasters, they attract immense public attention. A crash strikes quixotically, when most investors are fully committed to the market and a plunge in prices is the last thing they anticipated. Conversely, when everyone thinks the market is going to collapse, it probably won't.

The drama and surprise of a major crash stuns most investors: the majority will naturally be intensely shocked and may experience a high level of aversion to debt or any further ideas on investing. So when the blood is literally running in the street, although this is the best time to find great bargains, the bargain hunters are notoriously scarce.

A crash does not come knocking at the front door by appointment.
Jim Slater

The most important thing [about a crash] is that people do not expect it.
Jim Slater

It is only during a crash that the virtues or otherwise of playing with a new set of rules become apparent.
Riding the Millennial Storm, *Nury Vittachi*

Most of the rationalisations for the Wall Street boom were foreshadowed in the run-up to the 1929 crash.
Samuel Brittan, 'Economic Viewpoint', Financial Times, 13 May 1999

I would look at the number of stocks advancing as opposed to those declining. At present, 27 out of 100 have gone up over the past 10 days. In a potential crash situation the ratio would be much, much higher.

Robin Griffiths, chief technical strategist at HSBC

When the ingredients are ready [for a crash] the trigger mechanism could be a random event.

Robin Griffiths

Crises

While crashes are relatively rare, the global investment community seems to feed on a diet of recurring crises. In general, these may be of little serious concern to long-term investors, but they can be useful if you want to do some portfolio housekeeping. At such times, you might consider selling investments that look dubious to reinvest the proceeds in more promising companies as most prices fall in response to a crisis that has given the majority a nasty bout of nervousness.

At the centre of each recent crisis has been a rigid exchange-rate regime that proved ultimately unsustainable.

Robert Rubin, US Treasury secretary, 1995 to 1999, New York Times

It is always vital in the midst of apparent disaster to try to spot the point where action matches problems to be solved.

'Fund Manager's Diary', Investors Chronicle

The atmosphere of profit and greed leads to the error of optimism. But when a crisis of confidence occurs, the investor is gripped by fear—the error of pessimism, if you like.

Riding the Millennial Storm, *Nury Vittachi*

In the developed world, thanks to all-rapid change, today's average citizen enjoys a higher standard of living than a king did 200 years ago. Only, more often than not, he is not enjoying it as much as he might as he is too worried that it might all disappear at the click of a mouse.

The Economist

Crowds

Most people feel safer as part of a crowd, but that camaraderie comes at a price: it seriously reduces your ability to achieve high returns. Understanding crowd psychology gives the smart investor a powerful edge. Many huge swings, both up and down, reach truly staggering extremes. It seems contradictory but the bumper gains arise by investing as the market recovers from an abrupt slump because you are buying ahead of the crowd. This action demands total commitment because the crowd creates the winners, as Peter Lynch cautions, 'The stock market demands conviction; it victimises the unconvinced.'

Gurus are emphatic that you must ignore the majority view as it is so often wrong. Invariably, the majority are in the wrong place at the wrong time, explaining why there are so few outstandingly successful investors. When the consensus view is strong, it is frequently wrong. The majority of people may share a view, but then, the majority of people never become rich.

A group of lemmings looks like a pack of individualists compared with Wall Street when it gets a concept in its teeth.
Warren Buffett

I am cautious about going against the herd;
I am liable to be trampled on.
George Soros

Sometimes, investment managers behave like lemmings. This must be the only business where you do something because the guy next door does it.
John Walton, manager of British Empire Securities & General Trust

Tracker funds are sensible, it seems to me, as long as they are a minority. But when everyone is investing in trackers, only one thing lies ahead: a brick wall.
Alistair Blair, Investors Chronicle

The key to making money is to second guess the herd.
William Essex, The Sunday Times

Two important clues on market timing come from studying crowd psychology and the flow of money.
Anthony Harris, The Times

I can calculate the motions of heavenly bodies, but not the madness of people.
Sir Isaac Newton, 1720. He sold shares in the South Sea Company in April 1720, making a profit of 100%, collecting £7,000, a substantial sum of money in 1720; but he then re-entered the market at the July peak, subsequently losing £20,000

5 Managing Risks and Losses

....

The theme of 'Managing Risks and Losses' links together these two pivotal elements of successful investing because a cavalier attitude to risks increases the possibility of losses. Managing both risks and losses is one of the great secrets for achieving a superior investment performance. Gurus and experts are virtually unanimous in rating it as a key skill investors must master. Essentially it involves weighing up the probabilities of an adverse outcome, so you are fully prepared if it arises. When you manage your money you are really controlling risk. Any method that gives you more control helps you manage risk.

Risks
....

The inevitable outcome of ignoring financial risk is a loss that is measurable in hard cash. However, you do not eliminate risk simply by handing your financial affairs to an expert. Listen to investment advice but be careful where you invest your money. If you are offered a financial scheme that sounds mouth-wateringly attractive—beware, these schemes are the most risky. An endless stream of financial scandals in Britain endorses the idea that early lessons in risk management pay off.

When you invest, reduce the risk of loss by lifting your time horizon for growth from five to ten years, or even longer, because evidence shows the longer you keep your money in the market, the lower the risk. Although the reward for taking on risk can be measured by the excess return since, in general, the greater the return the higher the risk, the secret for making money is to practise risk control.

Warren Buffett insists investing is only risky when you do not know what you are doing. The risks dimish as your knowledge grows, which is a powerful reason for long-term investing. Increasing your knowledge breeds confidence and increasing confidence reduces risk. There are plenty of ways to control risk once you start seriously considering it: stay flexible, do careful preparation before you act, avoid over-priced shares and wait for the most favourable opportunities.

It is tremendously good news that there are so many different ways to reduce risk. Nervous or novice investors can form a club with like-minded friends or colleagues or use collective funds (unit or investment trusts). Or you can buy units in a monthly savings scheme to avoid investing a lump sum at a peak. Choose a fund that matches your personal risk preference. If you are cautious, avoid single country funds. They are volatile and hence, more risky. A FTSE All-Share tracker holds over 800 shares, reducing the risk of a huge drop in any one share adversely affecting your investment. The gurus stress the secret of reducing risk lies in taking small losses while leaving the profits to run. We can judge the importance of risk management from the quantity of pithy advice about it.

Risk comes from not knowing what you are doing.
Warren Buffett

To carry one's eggs in a great number of baskets without having the time or opportunity to discover how many have holes in the bottom, is the surest way of increasing risk and loss.
John Maynard Keynes

An investment is simply a gamble in which you have managed to tilt the odds in your favour.
Peter Lynch

You do better to make a few large bets and sit back and wait ... There are huge mathematical advantages to doing nothing.
Charles Munger, Warren Buffett's business partner of many decades

Mainstream America delights in buying on tips, rumours, stories, and advisory service recommendations. In other words, they are willing to risk their hard-earned money on what someone else says, rather than on knowing for sure what they are doing themselves.
William O'Neil

By being very selective, you increase your chances of picking superior performers. You can also watch those stocks much more carefully, which is important in controlling risk.
William O'Neil

You can risk 1 per cent of your capital, you can risk 5 per cent, or you can risk 10 per cent, but you better realise that the more you risk, the more volatile the results are going to be.
Ed Seykota, futures trader

If there is no risk, we try to create some because risk and feeling alive are different sides of the same coin. Risk is what makes us alive.
New Trading Dimensions, *Bill Williams*

Risk is a turn-on in life. We are not interested in haphazard risk. We are talking about risk that produces research, allowing us to understand the markets better and to extract profits from our knowledge and understanding.
New Trading Dimensions, *Bill Williams*

The biggest risk you can ever take is not betting on yourself.
New Trading Dimensions, *Bill Williams*

Basically, when you get down to it, to make money, you need to have an edge [a system] and employ good money management [risk control].
Monroe Trout, futures trader

It is ironic that the English use the phrase 'as safe as houses' for anything that is quite beyond risk. In financial terms, houses are not 'as safe as houses'.
Riding the Millennial Storm, *Nury Vittachi*

The guys that are loading risk into the fund in the hope that, one year, they will produce spectacular growth are the ones to avoid.
Julian Coutts, investment risk director at Standard Life

Investment is all about risk and reward and therefore, if you have a stock with a higher yield, there is inevitably a catch.
Nick Train, investment fund manager, M&G Group

I accept that there is a degree of risk involved, but what I'm trying to do is to find high yielding shares where the market has overreacted to the risks involved, in other words, there is an anomaly in valuation.
Nick Train, investment fund manager, M&G Group

Past performance is no guide at all. The form books show that the majority of funds that perform well in one time period failed badly next time round.
Gordon Maw, Virgin Direct

Tracking the index does not avoid risks of a market fall but removes the risk of a fund manager getting it wrong.
Gordon Maw, Virgin Direct

I have continually witnessed examples of other people that I have known being ruined by a failure to respect risk. If you don't take a hard look at risk, it will take you.
Larry Hite, Mint Investment Management Company

I don't like the idea of working within a narrow area. I want to spread my risks and my expertise.
Malcolm 'Max' King, fund manager with J.O. Hambros & Partners

People perceive equity investments as risky. But the performance statistics prove that deposit accounts are the real gamble.
Anne McMeehan, director of communications at Autif (Association of Unit Trusts and Investment Funds)

For an ailing portfolio, there has to be an exposure to the newer growth sectors. This introduces a great deal of risk, because the ratings are often speculative and bad news can cause heavy instant drops in share prices.
Barry Riley, Financial Times

In essence, the assertion that Wall Street is overvalued is a statement about the level of risk, not about where things will go next.
Leader article, Financial Times, *1 June 1996*

Trackers are fully exposed to stock market risk as well as reward. When the market falls, they will drop with it.
James Macintosh, Financial Times

In a bear market high-beta stocks do indeed justify their risky status, by falling more than low-beta ones. In bull markets [like the present—summer 1996] that simple truth tends to be neglected, to be rediscovered painfully each time.
Peter Martin, Financial Times

In thinking about risk you ought to look at the whole portfolio, not at each risk in isolation.
John Kay, Financial Times

Assume the odds being offered are ones at which the other side expects to make money.
John Kay, Financial Times

The financial economist contends that few of us really understand the concept of probability which underpins any systematic analysis of risk.
John Kay, Financial Times

Spreading the risk means spreading rewards thinner too.
Graham Searjeant, The Times

Risk is usually defined as the extent to which returns—including dividends as well as capital growth—fluctuate around their average level.
Investors Chronicle

The point of investment is to insure yourself against risks.
Investors Chronicle

Market discipline will work only if creditors bear the
consequences of the risks they take.
Robert Rubin, US Treasury secretary, 1995 to 1999, New York Times

A lot of people criticise Formula One as an unnecessary
risk. But what would life be like if we only did what's
necessary?
Niki Lauda, Formula One racing driver

I wouldn't do it if I didn't think we'd survive. That's what
we're preparing for in training—we think of the worst-
case scenarios and work out what we'd do, so that with
luck we'll never have to face anything we haven't
prepared for to some extent.
Richard Branson, on his round-the-world balloon challenge, December 1998

I think money that sits in the bank is just dead. If you are
not taking risks your life grinds to a halt.
Howard Jones, song writer of the hit 'Things can only get better'

To put two big companies together, you're actually risking
a hell of a lot, because you could argue there's no need to
do it at all.
Sir Richard Sykes, chairman of Glaxo Wellcome

Buying at regular intervals eliminates the risk of over-
investing at a stock market peak.
Quentin Lumsden, editor, Chart Breakout

To make a lot of money from taking risks you must expect
to lose a fair amount reasonably often.
Martin Taylor, during the period when he was chief executive at Barclays Bank

The rational judgement that the greater their number the greater the risk is likely to be submerged by the mere contagion of confidence which persuades him that the greater the numbers the more safely he himself may venture.
F. Lavington, The Trade Cycle

It's impossible to take an unnecessary risk. Because you only find out whether a risk was unnecessary after you've taken it.
Giovanni Agnelli, president of Fiat

The rewards of risk-bearing are so high as almost to eliminate the risk itself.
John Kay, Peter Moores director of the Said Business School at Oxford University

Respect the privilege of money and never forget that only real risk can provide true reward.
Matthew Harding, insurance tycoon and former director of Chelsea Football Club

Losses

Unless you have a lucky Midas touch, most quick ways of making money turn out to be quick ways of losing it. If lost pride accompanies a financial loss, it can be even tougher to swallow. One big loss can be more than a financial disaster if it damages your self-confidence. Yet from the comments on losses by gurus and experts we see that no one, not even the most sophisticated, brilliant investors, can avoid the occasional errors and hence losses.

Think positively: turn your losses into assets by learning from the personal investment errors you make. Face up to the fear of making losses by reading how gurus cope. In general they agree that taking small losses makes the greatest impact on portfolio success. This proves doubly beneficial if you run profits in companies with excellent growth prospects.

I compare cutting losses with owning an insurance policy. The loss is the small premium I pay to stay with the winners. Unless you use options or futures, which can be risky, small losses are the only available insurance for private investors. They are cheap insurance while you wait for the big profits to arrive. By taking small losses you may protect yourself from the occasional big ones.

When you start picking more winners than losers, you know you are making progress. As the redoubtable Peter Lynch reminds us, 'If seven out of ten stocks perform as expected, that's good going ... but six out of ten is all it takes to produce a very favourable return.'

There are only three rules on investing: first, never lose any money, second, never lose any money, and third, never lose any money.
Warren Buffett

Better to miss a lot than to lose a lot.
Dr Marc Faber

There is no shame in losing money on a stock. Everyone does it. What is shameful is to hold on to a stock, or, worse, buy more of it, when the fundamentals are deteriorating.
Peter Lynch

Take small losses. Profits always take care of themselves. But losses never do.

Jesse Livermore

The way you lose money in the stock market is to start off with an economic picture.

Peter Lynch, quoted in The New Money Masters *by John Train*

The average friend, stockbroker, or advisory service could be a source of losing advice.

William O'Neil

The secret of winning in the stock market does not include being right all the time. In fact, you should be able to win even if you are right only half the time. The key is to lose the least amount of money possible when you are wrong.

William O'Neil

The first rule of investing is not to lose any capital.

Investment Biker, *Jim Rogers*

My early losses taught me a lot. Since then—I don't like to say this kind of thing—I have made very few mistakes. I learned quickly not to do anything unless you know what you are doing. I learned that it is better to do nothing and wait until you get a concept right, and a price so right, that even if you are wrong, it is not going to hurt you.

Jim Rogers

Whenever I buy or sell anything, I always try to make sure I'm not going to lose any money first.

Jim Rogers

There is no such thing as a paper loss. A paper loss is a very real loss.

Jim Rogers

There are innumerable ways to lose money in rare coins.
John Train

They are always saying that the market is down because of profit taking. I think it would be wonderful if everybody was always taking profits. But, the truth is, most people make losses, and the reason markets go down is because they take their losses.
Mark Weinstein, independent investor

The real reason that most traders lose consistently is that they are fitting new information into old, inappropriate categories.
New Trading Dimensions, *Bill Williams*

In the 18 months since it sold its first toy on-line, eToys has attracted 365,000 customers. In the year to March [1999] it notched up $30 million in sales. Never mind the $30 million in losses to date.
Lex Column, Financial Times

The world is full of schemes aimed at parting the gullible from their money.
Clay Harris, Financial Times

Getting stuck in a losing venture is the worst kind of money pain there is.
Susan Garner

When your broker says it can only go one way, he means down.
Timothy Leary, of 1960s flower power fame

A recession is when your neighbor loses his job and a depression is when you lose yours.
Harry Truman, President of the United States of America (1945–52)

6 Valuation Teasers

I have called this next major theme 'Valuation Teasers', as valuing companies is quite problematic for many investors. Judging share valuations can be tricky. If it were not, then prices would surely not fluctuate as much as they do. Japan, for example, is often cited as a market that departs dramatically from fundamental valuation yardsticks used in Europe and America. The sections grouped under this theme are values, valuations and prices.

Values

Lord Darlington, in *Lady Windermere's Fan*, by Oscar Wilde, famously described a cynic as 'A man who knows the price of everything and the value of nothing.' In similar vein, we could say a value investor is 'someone who knows when the price of a company ignores hidden value'. Such investors are notorious for bargain basement invest-ment shopping rather than searching for 'high growth' companies. Reputedly, they scan the lists for successful companies selling at rock-bottom prices. Benjamin Graham is the most celebrated value investor in history. His disciples adhere to his philosophy although each has his own special modifications. Ironically, there is a paradox, as Warren Buffett explains; 'Growth', he insists, 'is simply the calculation used to determine value'. Although famed as a value investor, Warren Buffett owns huge share-holdings in some of America's biggest growth companies, not least of which is an 11 per cent holding in American Express and 8 per cent in Coca-Cola.

For ordinary investors, however, some of the 'bargains' they unearth may turn into pending disasters. Some great value investments are those where management develop a winning strategy to eliminate the problems that origin-ally made them 'bargains'. Even if management cannot improve a company's fortunes, shares trading on a discount to asset value can become lucrative bid targets. However, recovery shares often make me nervous. Yes, they are fantastic bargains—but only if they recover.

Growth is simply the calculation used to determine value.
Warren Buffett

You never know. You never know that valuations are high, by historic standards. You know the level of speculation is high, by any historic standards, and you know that it doesn't go on forever. But you don't know when it ends.
Warren Buffett, March 1999

If there is very good value, then I'm probably not going to lose much money even if I'm wrong.
Jim Rogers

If a business is worth a dollar and I can buy it for 40 cents, something good may happen to me.
Walter Schloss, a Buffett contemporary and fellow Benjamin Graham disciple

Finally, there comes the magical stage: People are so hysterical to buy, because they know that the market is going to go up forever, and prices exceed any kind of rational, logical economic value.
Jim Rogers

There is no way a company such as On-line can be at the valuation it was. The rise in the share price was, I think, due to a combination of massive investor ignorance, profit-taking and people jumping on the band wagon.
Nick Gibson, stockbroker at Durlacher

Value investing has not paid off in the past few years and I cannot promise that 1999 will be any different.
Barry Riley, Financial Times

The rise in the value of internet stocks has been described as irrational optimism, a mass delusion and a confidence trick. Such words barely capture the sheer exuberance of the internet world.
Roger Taylor and John Labate, Financial Times

Much analysis of stocks and sectors is focused not on the value (or lack of it) they offer but on who 'underowns' or 'overowns' them relative to market weightings.
Barry Riley, Financial Times

Value investors seek shares that are unappreciated by the market and look cheap relative to their assets, earnings or dividend yield.
Philip Coggan, FT Quarterly Review of Personal Finance

Value investing tends to be more popular in the UK, for the rather sad reason that Britain produces few truly dynamic companies.
Philip Coggan, FT Quarterly Review of Personal Finance

Obviously, interest rates are not the sole determinant of currency values; otherwise, the easiest trade in the world would be to sell the Japanese yen, where interest rates are virtually zero, and buy the Russian rouble, where bonds yield around 38 per cent.
Philip Coggan, Financial Times

The highest-value companies are simply those the market believes have the highest profit potential.
James Macintosh, Financial Times

A good manager is considered to be one who is right 55 per cent of the time. On this basis, it will take 160 years to be statistically certain whether such a fund manager is adding value.
Barry Riley, 'Weekend Money', Financial Times

Once in every cycle value is bound to have a bad year as investors fear an earnings slow-down and shift towards growth stocks.
Barry Riley, Financial Times

When the likes of British Gas, Hanson, BTR and British Telecom are suffering a permanent loss of shareholder value, value investors must beware; perhaps another layer of analysis and screening is required.
Barry Riley, Financial Times

The destruction of the value of money was the principal long-term bequest of the Keynesian era.
Martin Wolf, Financial Times

If the investment community as a whole chases big stocks, those stocks are likely to rise in value. And if they are going to rise in value, investors want to be in them.
Robert Cole, 'Tempus', The Times

Market capitalisation is an effective measurement as it shows the value of a company as dictated by shareholders alone, and, because the top 100 firms remain highly liquid, shifts in investor sentiment can be detected in a company's value.

Mark King, Money Observer, *December 1998*

Consider the numbers: 2% growth over 30 years gives an 80% increase in the value of a capital sum; 10% growth over 30 years gives a 1645% increase. We are talking about a difference of 20 times. It is scarce wonder that people might have been confused about real values during the inflationary process.

Roger Bootle, economist

Technology companies should be valued at a discount to the shares of companies like Disney and Coca-Cola, which have long-term earnings.

Bill Gates, co-founder and chief executive of Microsoft

We (my brothers and I) grew up in what we thought was a poor home, but we grew up in a very rich home, because what our parents did for us was give us values. And that's the legacy—not money.

Morton Mandel, chief executive, Premier Farnell

Valuations

Misjudgements are two-a-penny when it comes to valuing shares. The market for stocks would come to a grinding halt if everyone had the same views on valuations. Bill Williams, the American futures trader, has a wonderful twist on this market truism. 'The primary purpose of the market is to find immediately the exact price where there is an equal disagreement on value and an agreement on *price*.' Buyers and sellers make a market, but how disconcerting it is to recall that when they strike a deal, they have totally opposite views on valuations.

I think it pays excellent returns to learn the fundamental yardsticks of valuation. Knowing them gives you an edge and can help in the search for undervalued bargains.

- UK shares are thought to be cheap if the ratio of dividend yield of equities to bonds is below 2.
- UK shares are cheap if the dividend yield on the FTSE All-Share index is over 4.
- Look for shares with a low P/E and a high dividend yield.

Routine valuation measures do not apply to 'blue sky' shares. These are companies with superb new ideas or technologies, which involve early risks while they get established in their markets and start making profits. It is an astonishing fact that several of the largest American internet quoted companies and some huge start-up telecommunications companies listed on the UK's FTSE 100 index have only sales revenues and losses to report. In 1929, Radio Corporation of America (RCA) was a typical blue-sky share of its day. The ten-year-old radio industry enjoyed a phenomenal boom. RCA had never paid a dividend, yet managed to reach the amazing price of $114 a share at the September peak before plunging down to just a few dollars during the October crash.

Stocks are like anything else. You can't buy the best quality at the cheapest price!
William O'Neil

I look upon the market's mood as a kind of pendulum which swings to and fro across either side of real value.
Jim Slater

Fund flows have been one of the pillars in a market where valuation hasn't mattered.
Melissa Brown, a technical analyst at Prudential Securities Ltd., August 1996

Markets often get emotional as they reach tops and bottoms, and when they do, valuations often get pushed aside.
Gail Dudack, a market strategist at UBS Securities

We are driven by looking at valuations and going against conventional wisdom.
Tony Dye, chief investment officer at Philips & Drew

Investors should make sure that in valuing a company which possesses a proprietory technology they are not exaggerating the portion of the company's earnings to which that price protection applies.
Financial Times

The trouble with arguments about valuation is that markets often remain overvalued for months or even years.
Leader article, Financial Times, *1 June 1996*

In the wilder fringes of the new issues market, cynical company promoters reckon the less the punters understand about a company, the more it will be worth. Value is harder to spot, but it definitely still matters.
Barry Riley, 'Weekend Money', Financial Times

We really can't know whether the market is over-valued.
Tim Cogley, economist at the San Francisco Fed, May 1999

Within minutes of its (eToys) initial public offering (20 May 1999), investors had valued the group at $8 billion, a third more than Toys Я Us.
Lex Column, Financial Times

In the end, all equity valuations depend on earnings.
'Fund Manager', Investors Chronicle

When there is no inflation and little economic growth, any company that has the secret of growing its earnings can expect a high market valuation.
'Fund Manager', Investors Chronicle

Today's arguments about Internet valuations are identical to those heard in the Netherlands during the tulip mania and in Japan during the bubble economy of the eighties.
Anatole Kaletsky, The Times

Companies such as Amazon.com, Dell, Yahoo! and AOL have no proprietory technologies, operate in industries with very low barriers to entry and enjoy only marginal brand loyalty. Just as there is no rational limit to their valuation on the way up, there will be no rational floor to how far they can fall on the way down.
Anatole Kaletsky, The Times

Prices

Like Bonnie and Clyde, price and value are almost inseparable: you can't imagine one without the other. If you cannot judge value, you might easily get sucked into buying highly priced shares. Understanding how to value companies is therefore crucial. As the fund manager from *Investors Chronicle* observes, 'a company's earnings decide the fate of its share price'. When companies make innovative products, expand into new markets, appoint aggressive new management or undergo restructuring, with or without mergers or takeovers, investor enthusiasm sends the share price racing. There is nothing quite so exhilarating as the buzz you get when the market re-rates a share you hold because it has woken up to the company's bright prospects you cleverly anticipated months before.

We try to price, rather than time, purchases.
Warren Buffett

The P/E will tell you how many years it will take to get back your initial investment. An extremely high P/E is a handicap to a stock as it requires incredible earnings to justify the high price.
Peter Lynch

It's like the gold rush. When people see a good thing they rush in and push prices up too far.
Jim Rogers

The perennial rise in stock prices is not automatic; it is created by the reinvestment of company cash flow.
John Train

Astronomic price earnings ratios rarely last for long, as they thrive on excessive hope and for that reason the most has to be made of them while they persist.
Jim Slater, Analyst, September 1990

I firmly believe that for every good thing in life, there's a price you have to pay.
Monroe Trout, futures trader

The primary purpose of the market is to find immediately the exact price where there is an equal disagreement on value and an agreement on price.
Bill Williams

This kind of short-term obsession about earnings, where one quarter's disappointment can mean giving up 20 per cent or more of the share price, illustrates to me how fragile are the underpinnings of this market.
Michael Metz, investment strategist at Oppenheimer & Co

You learn by experience what drives share prices, and we use everything available.
Phillipa Gould, manager of Hill Samuel's Japan-oriented unit trusts

Tracking the relationship between equity prices and gilt yields is not a job for the faint-hearted.
Debbie Harrison, Financial Times

After three successive reductions in interest rates last autumn, a great deal of asset price inflation has, so to speak, passed over the bridge.
John Plender, Financial Times

Bulls like to be in a minority, with most of the players in the market worrying that stock valuations are too high. That's likely to improve the chances of even higher prices being achieved.
'Fund Manager', Investors Chronicle

7 Prospecting For Success

Several key strands in the quest for investment success are linked together under the theme, 'Prospecting for Success'. The topics cover information, research, forecasts, exercising patience, preparation and analysis. Finally, there are a few quotes on fear and failure.

Gurus have incisive views on these subjects to help us garner some of the quintessential elements of success.

Information and Research

With the explosion of new web sites and growing availability of financial journals there is a danger of 'information overload'. Unfortunately, knowing what information you are looking for is not the same as being able to lay your hands on it. When I began, I did not even know where to find suitable investment books. Today, there is a plethora of choice.

Even as a raw recruit, I realised buying good information is a precious resource not to be lightly tossed away. Filing newspaper cuttings and articles on companies you own or might buy shares in soon earns its keep. At the outset, I had a miser's approach to buying information. Yet while my outlay on information was modest, my frugality was inordinately expensive in time and effort.

Now it seems obvious that acquiring sound information is the downpayment for making big profits.

This may be the age of information but reliable information is still a scarce commodity. One source too easily overlooked is the company itself: a rich repository of meaningful facts for inquisitive investors. The gurus acknowledge the pivotal role of information.

Although this *Treasury* does not hold a large number of quotations on research, I greatly value those that are included. I believe time spent researching companies is never wasted. William O'Neil is scathing on how easily the average American investor is swayed towards buying on tips, rumours, stories and other people's advice but ignores the crucial element of personal research. His remarks underlie the inherent risks: 'In other words, they are willing to risk their hard-earned money on what someone else says, rather than on knowing for sure what they are doing themselves.'

Time spent on research is like a piece of string—it can be as long or as short as you prefer but there is no point in re-inventing the wheel when there is so much available knowledge from gurus.

Avoid 'inside information' as you would the plague.
Philip Carret, quoted in The New Money Masters *by John Train*

I knew the more I understood about the company, the better off I would be.
Benjamin Graham

Investors can beat stock performance benchmarks using publicly available information.
Jim Slater

No matter what information you have, no matter what you are doing, you can be wrong.
Larry Hite, Mint Investment Management Company

Investment is riddled with paradoxes. For instance, the better the flow of information and analysis, the more difficult it is for any individual to shine.
Barry Riley, 'Weekend Money', Financial Times

You're neither right nor wrong because other people agree with you. You're right because your facts are right and your reasoning is right—and that's the only thing that makes you right.
Warren Buffett, recalling advice he got from his tutor, Benjamin Graham

Focus on those things you want least to happen and on what your response should be.
William Eckhardt, futures trader

If you're worried, channel that energy into research.
William Eckhardt, futures trader

Investing without research is like playing stud poker and never looking at the cards.
One Up on Wall Street, Peter Lynch

The secret of getting rich from investing is to go your own way, do your own research and make up your own mind.
Jim Rogers

Do not be persuaded to act against your judgement—so long as you have done your research properly.
William Essex, The Sunday Times

We are a research-based house, and the forty stocks in the portfolio are basically the forty best ideas we have at any one time.
Jim Cox, investment manager of Schroder's UK Enterprise unit trust

A lot of time and energy has to be put into it [stock selection]. You might have to research ten before you get one that's suitable.
Nick Train, investment fund manager, M&G Group

Later Marx was to recall his mother's shrewd words, 'If only Karl had made capital instead of writing about it'.
Wives of Fame, Edna Healey, (on Jenny, wife of Karl Marx)

Research is to see what everybody else has seen, and to think what nobody else has thought.
Albert Szent-Gyorgyi, biology Nobel prize winner in 1937 for discovering Vitamin C

Forecasts

Goodhart, a former chief economist at the Bank of England, had a law named after him: Goodhart's Law says that any stable relationship breaks down once it is relied upon for forecasting. This is unfortunate because relying on luck is not a sensible way to prepare for the future: better to follow a realistic route, even when forecasting seems more like wishful thinking than inspired judgement.

Yet even if history doesn't exactly repeat itself, it comes surprisingly close at pivotal times, especially in the stock market where memories of previous extremes drop out of the collective memory every ten years or so, if we ignore the mega-crashes with around fifty- to sixty-year repetitions.

Of course, as everyone knows, the past is not a reliable guide to the future, but with the right frame of mind, you can see tantalising glimpses of the big picture. If you spot the over-arching mega-trends, you will be more in tune with the future.

In the 1920s, investor imagination fed on motor and air travel, electricity, still an exciting novelty, and the brilliant future offered by film studios and radio. Modern equivalents are discernible in biotechnology, telecommunications, mobile telephony and the internet. Some of them may one day become outstanding investments.

The greatest success comes from spotting winning trends early, but forecasts of future earnings are precisely that—predictions and, therefore, unreliable. Hence, it is doubly fascinating to learn what gurus and experts say about forecasting, since so much of their expertise unquestionably lies in visualising the future long before the rest of us have even begun to factor it into our plans.

The only value of stock forecasters is to make fortune tellers look good.
Warren Buffett

I also spend fifteen minutes a year on where the stock market is going.
Peter Lynch, quoted in The New Money Masters *by John Train*

People's confidence in their ability to predict secular trends has greatly diminished.
Michael Steinhardt, Steinhardt Partners

With long-term interest rates at 5.5% there are a lot of
questions about whether returns on equity can remain
at 18%–20%. A lot of companies are implicitly promising
you those returns will continue, but I am dubious about
those claims.
Warren Buffett

The farther one gets away from Wall Street the more
scepticism one will find as to the pretensions of stock
market forecasting or timing.
Benjamin Graham

Technology is extremely hard to forecast.
Ralph Wanger, quoted in The New Money Masters *by John Train*

History counsels us that sharp changes in direction are
rarely, if ever, anticipated.
Alan Greenspan, chairman of the US Federal Reserve Board, May 1999

Despite the remarkable progress witnessed to date, we
have to be quite modest about our ability to project the
future of technology and its implications for productivity
growth and for the broader economy.
Alan Greenspan, chairman of the US Federal Reserve Board, May 1999

What makes this business so fabulous is that, while you
may not know what will happen tomorrow, you can have
a very good idea what will happen over the long run.
Larry Hite, of Mint Investment Management Company

You have to understand what is happening in the US now
and appreciate that this [growth in IT usage] will be
repeated in other countries, just as it was with hamburgers
or mountain bikes.
Brian Ashford-Russell, director and manager of Henderson Technology

The forecaster, although his job is to give flesh to intangible hunches, tends to be the person who knows how few hard-and-fast rules there are in life.

Riding the Millennial Storm, *Nury Vittachi*

Every investor is an amateur forecaster, and few realise how tough a game they are playing.

Riding the Millennial Storm, *Nury Vittachi*

Hindsight would again have been a better guide: it shows that major market trends, be they in securities, property, or even exchange rates, always go much farther than reason suggests.

Anthony Harris, The Times

Wall Street gurus often shroud their predictions in enough mist that they later can claim they were right, no matter what happens.

John R. Dorfman, staff reporter, Wall Street Journal, *European edition*

At some point in the next five years, the trackers are surely due for their comeuppance. They may take the rest of us with them.

Alistair Blair, Investors Chronicle

Contrary to media hype, inflation is not dead. It will rise again, just like Lazarus.

David Roche, 'Weekend Money', Financial Times

Study the past, if you would divine the future.

Confucius

One has to establish a view about where the statistics are leading. One has to anticipate an uncertain future. Gut feelings and experience play a considerable role.

Professor Charles Goodhart, London School of Economics

There are two sorts of forecasters. Those who don't know, and those who don't know they don't know.

J.K. Galbraith, American economist

The herd-like instinct of forecasters—who can blame you for being wrong when everyone else is also wrong?—make it a dangerous business to rely on a projection merely because it represents a consensus.

Irwin Stelzer, The Sunday Times

Patience

Most private investors realise it needs colossal patience to stay in a share, waiting for the big surge to arrive. Patience is equally relevant when waiting for the really worthwhile investment opportunities to occur. Gurus emphasise the importance of waiting patiently for the best chances of making truly fantastic gains: they crop up regularly, for those who are willing to become serious students of investment.

When Warren Buffett quips, 'Lethargy bordering on sloth remains the cornerstone of my investment style', he is reminding impatient novices of how long it takes to find a superb investment idea. He advises exercising patience until that opportunity emerges—then sit back and allow it to give you a resounding success.

Arguably, today we live in the most 'instant-oriented' society ever: we have instant coffee, tea and soup, plus instant communications, even instant families if you marry a divorcee with children. In such a climate it is difficult to recall that success in anything takes time. I particularly like

Eddie Cantor's witticism: 'It takes years to make an overnight success.' This popular American 1920s singer cleverly salvaged some of his capital by selling his shares a few days before the Wall Street crash.

Peter Lynch has beguiling baseball analogies of 'ten-baggers'. They apply to company shares that grow ten-fold while you are holding them. When you choose a small growth share for its outstanding prospects, you must stay faithful to your judgement otherwise, when the market eventually wakes up to its charms, you may not still be on board. Many gurus are adamant that excellent stock-picking techniques only bring success for those prepared to be patient.

It is true, unfortunately, that the modern organisation of the capital market requires, for the holder of quoted equities, much more nerve, patience and fortitude than the holder of wealth in other forms.
John Maynard Keynes

Recoveries take time.
Richard Hughes, Manager of M&G's Recovery split-capital trust

We tend to invest on a three-year view, and it doesn't worry us if the shares go down in the short term.
John McClure, investment manager, Guinness Flight

The most common question I'm asked is: 'Should I be doing something about this?' Unless it's very obvious what's happening, the answer is to wait.
Bill Tatham, Towry Law International

How much you are prepared to invest in smaller companies depends upon the time scale you are looking at. I think it makes sense to have that smaller company bias if you are prepared to take a longer term view.
Paul Whitney, head of NatWest Investment Management

Sometimes in markets, watching, though frustrating, is better than plunging in with inadequate conviction as to the correct strategy to follow.
'Fund Manager', Investors Chronicle

But often in the past I have found that patience works, even if the trick becomes one of making money out of the delay.
'Fund Manager', Investors Chronicle

It takes years to make an overnight success.
Eddie Cantor, the popular American 1920s singer

One must know how to await opportunities, and never be tempted to precipitate events.
Prince Victor Napoleon, great nephew to Napoleon

Preparation and Analysis

I personally think success in investing is not really a game of chance or luck, like roulette. It depends crucially on preparation. I think detailed preparation is a powerful antidote to the fear of losing money in poor investments. Investing can be a gamble, so hedge the bets more heavily in your favour by careful preparation. As there are very few quotations on preparation, I assume the gurus think it is too obvious, and essential to success, even to warrant discussion.

Analysis covers a wide gamut of topics: timing, technical analysis of the market, plus trends. The gurus and experts offer useful ideas on these varied subjects. I rely on technical analysis as an aid to making buy and sell decisions, but most of the greatest gurus who are long-term investors rely solely on fundamental analysis because their knowledge of company statistics is so profound. For speculators and futures traders, however, following charts and technical factors is a central part of their analytical armoury. William O'Neil, a growth investor, thinks ignoring price movement evidence on charts is like doctors trying to diagnose chest complaints without looking at the X-rays, but this is a minority view among gurus. He makes impressive arguments for why private investors should consider technical analysis, as they need to harness as much useful information as possible. Small investors may not be able to acquire all the fundamental information that is fed to professionals, but if you take the trouble to understand the concepts, technical analysis is readily available to everyone.

Yet no single indicator is infallible. Technical indicators are rather like buses: they work best when they turn up in groups. The choicest opportunities arise when several indicators give the same signal together. While price action looks erratic, even directionless, there are periods when markets do become more orderly, displaying structures that override the frequent ambiguity. Structure occurs every-where in the markets: in base-formations, trading ranges, breakouts, rectangles, channels, flags, support and resistance levels and, of course, trends. If you can master the insights offered by technical signals, you give yourself a valuable edge.

The famous speculator, Jesse Livermore, made a fortune using price breakouts on Wall Street in the early part of the twentieth century. He described market drift as 'the get-nowhere prices'. As the majority of investors rely primarily on fundamental analysis, those who use technical analysis should have an advantage, by separating themselves from the crowd.

Some of the best buy signals occur as a new trend begins. It can be foolhardy to bet against the trend, as George Soros muses, 'Most of the time we are punished if we go against the trend'. Some of the most powerful trends last for weeks, months, years, even decades. Many invest-ment themes converge when discussing trends, purely because the trend is such a remarkable source of superb profits. Patience, research, technical analysis, timing, forecasting, all play a role in securing the maximum benefit from the emergence of a trend. Gurus know that staying with the trend produces the outstanding results that lift them way above the investment crowds.

A buy and hold strategy excels when a strong trend is running. This is unbelievably exhilarating when it occurs in a share you are holding. Ignoring the big trend or jump-ing in and out to catch the fluctuations is as frustrating as chasing clouds, but after a substantial trend has developed, the reversal can be alarmingly dramatic.

If you aren't willing to own a share for ten years, then don't own it for ten minutes.
Warren Buffett

How would I feel if I put my family's net worth in it?
Warren Buffett

Preparation is everything. Noah did not start building the ark when it was raining.
Warren Buffett

The inevitable never happens. It is the unexpected always.
John Maynard Keynes

Great opportunities occur every year in America. Get yourself prepared and go for it. You will find that little acorns can grow into giant oaks.
William O'Neil

The best judgement we can make about managerial competence does not depend on what people say, but simply what the record shows.
Warren Buffett

To invest successfully over a lifetime does not require a stratospheric IQ, unusual business insights or inside information. What is needed is a sound intellectual framework for making decisions and the ability to keep emotions from corroding that framework.
Warren Buffett

Charts provide valuable information about what is going on that cannot be obtained easily any other way. They allow you to follow a huge number of different stocks in an organised manner.
William O'Neil

High volume at a key point is an extraordinarily valuable tip-off that a stock is ready to move.
William O'Neil

Most investors think that charts are hocus-pocus. Only
about 5 to 10 per cent of investors understand charts.
William O'Neil

I don't have time to get out the charts and show you how
the world works.
Jim Rogers to CNBC-TV's 'Squark Box' host, Mark Haines

Sometimes the chart for a market will show an incredible
spike either up or down. You will see hysteria in the charts.
Jim Rogers

The trend is your friend most of the way; trend followers
only get hurt at inflection points, where the trend changes.
George Soros

Most of the time we are punished if we go against the
trend. Only at an inflection point are we rewarded.
George Soros

The fact that I increased investments in internet
companies—and held them as their prices rose quickly in
the fourth quarter [of 1998]—was due at least as much to
my feel for the psychology surrounding these stocks as it
was to any numbers-related analysis.
Robert Stansky, manager of Fidelity's flagship, Magellan Fund

More and more people are paying attention to market
timing, not that they are necessarily qualified to do it
terribly well, but because they have come to realise what a
buy-and-hold approach means.
Michael Steinhardt, Steinhardt Partners

Although Wall Street is heading for a big fall at some
stage, there is still scope for the timing to tantalise us.
Barry Riley, Financial Times

We have recommended PDFM [a fund management subsidiary of Union Bank of Switzerland, now renamed Philips & Drew] to clients because it has a clear investment discipline and sticks consistently to that discipline.
Nathan Gelber, managing director of Stamford Associates,
a pension funds consultant

There is a lot of glib talk that says in order to make money you have to be fully invested in the market at all times, but this is rubbish. Market timing can make all the difference.
Paul Walton, UK equity strategist at Goldman Sachs

Put simply, it's time that counts, not timing.
Richard Branson, boss of Virgin

Personal pension investment is like cooking. Using good ingredients is not enough; getting the timing right is important too.
Jonathan Guthrie, FT Quarterly Review of Personal Finance,
July 19 and 20 1996

Mercury Asset Management's investment policy is to pick companies that it believes are undervalued and invest in them heavily. That makes it prone to being the arbiter of bid battles.
John Gapper, Financial Times

You need the right tools to decide which are good and bad investment opportunities in those areas where you do appreciate the business.
Investors Chronicle

The finances of France are in a deplorable state and I would never have accepted responsibility for them if my own were not in an equally shaky condition.
Charles-Alexandre de Calonne, on his appointment by Louis XVI as
Controller-General of Finances in 1783

As share prices have risen beyond levels that make sense in terms of income, history, inflation or earnings prospects, the measures that make share prices look expensive have been ruthlessly supressed in fund managers' minds.

Graham Searjeant, The Times

Fear and Failure

Fear and failure can both be key concerns for investors who have yet to find a winning strategy. For inexperienced investors fear of failure draws the two even closer. I treat planning for failure as a form of insurance: as William Eckhardt sagely warns, 'Don't think about what the market's going to do; you have absolutely no control over that. Think about what you're going to do if it gets there'. Time spent analysing your failures can repay you many times. By thinking the unthinkable, that is, the chance of failure, you reduce that chance considerably.

Fear is one of the most powerful human emotions. Fear of the unknown can create raw panic, as in a crash. If you learn basic investment principles, you can avoid this fate. Something you know well is rarely a cause for fear. Zig Ziglar, an American trader, uses this telling description of fear: 'False Evidence Appearing Real'. I rely on another, equally memorable phrase that seems to capture the positive force of fear as an investment ally, 'The way to be safe is never to feel secure.'

Be most afraid when there is no fear.

John Train, Financial Times

Worldly wisdom teaches that it is better to fail conventionally than it is to succeed unconventionally.
John Maynard Keynes

Commitment is the psychic fuel that allows us to face our fears, to realise we cannot escape them, that to face them is to overcome them.
The Intuitive Trader, *Robert Koppel*

Fear loses its potency when the unknown suddenly becomes the familiar.
Philip Stephens, Financial Times

For now it is apparent that fear is widespread amongst investors and traders. They are the people who actually move prices.
'The Trader', Investors Chronicle

Markets do not usually go on discounting the same fears over and over.
'Options Trader', Investors Chronicle

People have nothing to fear from the stock market. Put it this way, you won't find many building society managers who invest their pension fund in a deposit account.
Anne McMeehan, Autif (Association of Unit Trusts and Investment Funds)

What makes people invest is not just tax relief but fear: when they're scared they'll run out of money in retirement, they'll save.
Stephen Lansdown, managing director of Hargreaves Lansdown

Panic has no nationality, and fear is not the property of any one people.
O Jerusalem! Larry Collins and Dominique Lapierre

8 Ride Up The Learning Curve

....

Grouped under the theme 'Ride up the Learning Curve' is a collection of topics spanning numerous steps for developing investment skills. They include the process of learning itself, acquiring knowledge and confidence, the vital skill of stock-picking, the role of investment systems and learning from mistakes. These topics excite plenty of comment from gurus and other savants.

Learning

....

However much you learn, there always seems more to know, but I see investing as very much a trial and error process—face the trials and learn from the errors. The experience of gurus is invaluable here, as learning from other people's mistakes is clearly far cheaper than learning from your own. There is no better way of learning than copying the great masters. Cut out a great deal of aggravation and expense by riding up the learning curve on the coat-tails of the gurus.

I've learned the perimeter of my circle of competence.
Warren Buffett

Soros has taught me that when you have tremendous conviction on a trade, you have to go for the jugular.
Stanley Druckenmiller, manager of the Soros funds

I'll tell you how I became a winner, I learned how to lose.
Martin Schwartz, American hedge fund manager

QUESTION *Jack Schwager:*
Do you remember what you learned in those early days?
ANSWER *Monroe Trout:*
I learned how quickly you can lose money if you don't know what you're doing.
Taken from New Market Wizards *by J. D. Schwager*

Learning from past mistakes is all very well, but there is always the danger with investments that one learns the wrong lessons.
Investors Chronicle

Experience keeps a dear school,
but fools will learn in no other.
Poor Richard's Almanac 1743

I forget what I was taught. I only remember what I've learnt.
Patrick White

Time is the great teacher, but unfortunately,
it kills all of its students.
Hector Berlioz

You cannot teach a man anything; you can only help him to find it within himself.
Galileo Galilei

Do not weep; do not wax indignant. Understand.
Baruch Spinoza

Man can learn nothing except by going from the known to
the unknown.
Claude Bernard

Knowledge

In the previous theme, we discussed the element of fear to
which investors are often prone—but knowledge is a
terrific antidote to fear. Moreover, self-knowledge is a
valuable addition to an investor's armoury. Sadly, I have
known investors who do not have a knack for making
profitable investments. When it comes to making big
profits, the person working hardest against them may be
themselves. Benjamin Graham puts this succinctly, 'An
investor's worst enemy is not the stock market but oneself'.
Every investor needs to examine his or her own investment
psyche from time to time. Is it wired for winning or losing?

It is clearly better to understand a little than to mis-
understand a lot, so that your investments grow alongside
your improving expertise. Jim Slater, with his intriguing
Zulu Principle, suggests how to become more knowledgeable about markets: 'as few people know very much about
Zulus, anyone who takes the trouble to study them can
become an expert'. So it is with investment skills, if you
focus your attention on one narrow sphere. Warren Buffett
calls this his 'circle of competence'. I tend to think my
investment edge depends on the extent to which *my*
knowledge of a promising situation exceeds that of the
market. I don't claim this is easy to achieve, but on the
occasions when it works, it is pure magic.

It is better to be certain of a good result than
hopeful of a great one.
Warren Buffett

An investor's success is in direct proportion to the degree
to which he or she understands the investment.
Warren Buffett

The market, like the Lord, helps those who help
themselves. But, unlike the Lord, the market does not
forgive those who know not what they do.
Warren Buffett

People know better, but when they hear a rumour—
particularly when they hear it from a high place—they
just can't resist the temptation to go along.
Warren Buffett

What counts for people in investing is not how
much they know, but how realistically they define
what they don't know.
Warren Buffett

Optimism means expecting the best, but confidence
means knowing how to handle the worst.
The Zurich Axioms, *Max Gunther*

When the facts change, I change my mind.
John Maynard Keynes

A lot of people would rather understand the market
than make money.
Ed Seykota, futures trader

I don't believe, I know.
Carl Jung

One's knowledge and experience are definitely limited and there are seldom more than two or three enterprises at any time in which I personally feel myself entitled to put full confidence.
John Maynard Keynes, letter to a business associate, 1934

To make money, you must find something that nobody else knows, or do something that others won't do because they have rigid mind-sets.
Peter Lynch, quoted in The New Money Masters *by John Train*

As a fund manager, I depended a great deal on my emotions. That was because I was aware of the inadequacy of my knowledge. The predominant feelings I operated with were doubt, uncertainty and fear.
George Soros, the philanthropic financier, president of the Quantum Funds

An investor who has all the answers doesn't even understand the questions.
Sir John Templeton

You should also understand that to win consistently in the markets you must get to know them and how they process incoming information.
New Trading Dimensions, *Bill Williams*

Grace is given of God, but knowledge is bought in the market.
Arthur Hugh Clough

We don't believe in operating with a minimum unit size. If we buy small amounts and build our knowledge up, when that company has a rights issue two years later we have two years of knowledge that other people don't have.
John McClure, investment manager, Guinness Flight

That's how I got started. Trying to understand it myself so that I could explain it to other people.

Pattie Dunn, chairman of Barclays Global Investors, the world's largest institutional fund manager

Knowledge is of two kinds. We know a subject ourselves or we know where we can find information upon it.

Dr Samuel Johnson

Buying a company without having sufficient knowledge of it may be even more dangerous than having inadequate diversification.

Common Stocks and Uncommon Profits, *Philip Fisher*

The person who knows that he doesn't know much, knows much.

Dr Marc Faber, quoted in Riding the Millennial Storm *by Nury Vittachi*

Diversification is a hedge for ignorance. I think you are much better off owning a few stocks and knowing a great deal about them.

William O'Neil

The trouble in this world is not caused by what people don't know, but what they do know that ain't so.

Josh Billings, American sage

The public do not know which are the low-charging companies and which are the high. About one million plans are sold each year, mostly to people who cannot judge what they are buying.

John Chapman, co-author of Kitemarking or Benchmarking? *New Policy Institute*

Stock-Picking and Systems

Finding a successful stock-picking system is the investor's search for the Holy Grail: it generates out-performance. For thousands of investors inspired stock-picking is their key to success. A brilliant stock-picker doesn't need to worry where the market is heading, but to amateur investors, market direction can matter a great deal. Whatever routine suits your personality, a flair for stock-picking helps winning investors sift out the real success stories from thousands of mediocre candidates. Jesse Livermore's idea of 'the get-nowhere prices' could as easily cover 'the get-nowhere companies'.

Stock-picking fits naturally with the idea of following a sound investment system: this is imperative for reaping fat rewards. Achieving an above average annual return on your investments becomes easier when you have a well thought-out investment system. We should utilise the fact that the human mind strives to find order although some people's desks, kitchens, bedrooms or offices might make you wonder if this really holds true. Yet most people have a natural urge to obey the demands of a set routine. When this desire is channelled around a reliable stock-picking system, the results can be electrifying.

Great stocks are extremely hard to find. If they weren't, then everyone would own them. I knew I wanted to own the best or none at all.

Philip Fisher, in conversation with Robert G. Hagstrom, 1998

I choose a company which can be run by an idiot because you can be sure that one day it will be.
Peter Lynch

Stock-picking is like gambling: those who win well, seldom bet, but when they do, they bet heavily.
Charles Munger

Essentially, I'm trying to find companies that have a real chance of being around in three years and dominate their niches.
Robert Stansky, manager of Fidelity's flagship, Magellan Fund

If you have too much money to run, even if all you do is pick stocks, you'll have less time to do a good job. And you won't be able to restrict yourself to the best situations.
Duncan Trinder, manager of Gartmore British Growth unit trust

You have to remember that share picking is a very difficult game. Effectively, you are bidding against the market.
Paul Whitney, head of NatWest Investment Management

An iron rule of stock-picking theories seems to be that, as soon as they become widely known, they cease to work.
Philip Coggan, 'Weekend Money', Financial Times

Stock-picking systems have an easily understood appeal. If one can find a set of hard and fast rules which select market winners, a lot of the anxiety can be removed from the investment process.
Philip Coggan, Financial Times

Hindsight is a wonderful thing, but how do you identify the next wonder stock?
Richard Waters, Financial Times

Stock selection is an art requiring a whole lot of detailed information.
Dominick Coyle, FT Quarterly Review of Personal Finance

All that investors have to do is pick the funds that will do well. Unfortunately, this is incredibly hard.
James Macintosh, Financial Times

Private investors keen to avoid having to get individual stock-picking correct need a combination of indexed portfolios and a selection of growth-oriented funds.
'Fund Manager', Investors Chronicle

Stock-picking is the only effective way to build long-term value in your portfolio.
'Fund Manager', Investors Chronicle

Investors should therefore be extremely careful as trying to buck that reversal of fortune (the arrival of a bear market) in the past with skilful stock-picking has proved to be a challenge beyond the talents of most mortals.
'Fund Manager', Investors Chronicle

So long as your fundamental stock selections are right, you should not be pressed into selling them on the grounds of a fleeting change in sentiment.
William Essex, The Sunday Times

There's very little money to be made recommending our strategy [buy-and-hold] ... Your broker would starve to death. Recommending something to be held for 30 years is a level of self-sacrifice you'll rarely see in a monastery, let alone a brokerage house.
Warren Buffett

Lethargy bordering on sloth remains the cornerstone of my investment style.
Warren Buffett

My dad's investment approach is based on an unusual but insightful notion that less is more [focus on only a few stocks, rather than on many].
Ken Fisher, son of Philip Fisher, in an interview with Robert G. Hagstrom, 1998

There is virtually no kind of situation that can't be handled with a system.
Robert R. Godfrey

I have over a period developed a set of standards for equity investment which have resulted in a very substantial capital appreciation being achieved during the last few years, at a time when share prices in general, have, at least for the past three years, on balance been declining.
Jim Slater, Sunday Telegraph, March 1963

The secret lies in only two factors—method and gearing. By gearing he means obtaining as much credit as possible from banks and brokers to give full scope to your method.
Article on Jim Slater, Analyst, September 1990

Start with the basics, select a system, work at it, read regularly, monitor results and keep striving to improve.
Jim Slater, Analyst, September 1990

The bottom line is that you need an edge. One of the ways you can get an edge is to find a successful system.
Monroe Trout, futures trader

I must create a system or be enslaved by another man's.
William Blake

More is learned from one's errors than from one's successes.
Primo Levi

Mistakes
....

Financial mistakes are invariably costly, but only if you never learn how to avoid repeating them. Mistakes are only expensive if you do not profit from the lessons that they teach. The gurus are impressively humble on the topic of mistakes. By using your mistakes wisely, they become a short-cut to future investment success.

_____

As far as the first half of 1987 was concerned, I was totally wrong. The year opened with a salvo.
Dr Marc Faber, 'The Gloom, Boom & Doom Report'

Still, I don't wish to be too harsh on anyone for having been too optimistic about the Asian region, since I have been totally wrong about so many other issues since I started in this business 27 years ago.
Dr Marc Faber

But you have to know when you are wrong. Then you sell. Most stocks I buy are a mistake.
Peter Lynch, quoted in The New Money Masters *by John Train*

It is a mistake to think one limits one's risks by spreading too much between enterprises about which one knows little and has no reason for special confidence.
John Maynard Keynes, letter to a business associate, 1934

The balance between confidence and humility is best learned through extensive experience and mistakes.
Michael Steinhardt, Steinhardt Partners

I have made so many decisions and mistakes that it has made me wise beyond my years as an investor.
Michael Steinhardt, Steinhardt Partners

There is a very good investor I speak to frequently who said, 'All I bring to the party is twenty-eight years of mistakes'. I really believe he is right. When you make a mistake, there is some subconscious phenomenon that makes it less likely for you to make that same mistake again.
Michael Steinhardt, Steinhardt Partners

For every difficult, intractable problem there's a solution that's neat, plausible and wrong.
H.L. Mencken

Some of the greatest blunders occur not through errors of fact, but errors of logic.
Roger Bootle

I've made many mistakes and miscalculations … on days when I'm wearing a tight collar.
How to be Rich, Paul Getty

I never blame others. To blame others is a sign of weakness.
General de Gaulle

A bad decision is when you know what to do and you don't do it.
Duncan Goodhew, Olympic gold medallist for Britain in 1980

9 Share-Search

....

Under the theme of 'Share-Search' we look at expressions
and quotations made by gurus and experts on companies
in general, on growth shares and on the pivotal concepts
underpinning sound investments.

General Companies
....

There is a treasure trove of small companies with giant
growth prospects, waiting to be discovered by the diligent
investment sleuth. There is no luck or mystery involved
in spotting successful companies; their shares rise because
they have a super story to tell. However, vigilance is
needed as companies, like investors, can get blown off
course. Warren Buffett lays great stress on the calibre of
management. For him, the winning company has a boss
he can believe in. So it pays to remember that when you
buy a share, you are backing the management.

It seems probable that stocks have been passing not so much
from the strong to the weak as from the smart to the dumb.
Colonel Ayres, October 1929

You don't get hurt by things that you don't own that go up.
It's what you do own that kills you.
Peter Lynch, quoted in The New Money Masters *by John Train*

There's nothing like owning a stock for giving you a
feeling for it.

George Michaelis, quoted in The New Money Masters *by John Train*

Land can sometimes be impossible to sell when you need
to sell it, whereas shares can always be sold at a price.

Jim Rogers

Brokers tell you that stocks will keep going up because it is
different this time. Never believe this. It is never different.

Jim Rogers

Equities move ahead in recessions.

John Templeton

There is a tremendous industry rationalising why equities
are so high.

Tony Dye, Financial Times, *September 1996*

The contribution of surging liquidity and decent earnings
momentum could act like rocket fuel for equities.

Peter Tasker, head of equity strategy at Kleinwort Benson, Tokyo

I look at shares where it hurts to look. Very often, the most
stunning opportunities are those where the negative vibes
are at a crescendo. It's front page news in the FT, there's a
profits warning, the shares halve in value, all the stuff you
don't want to see. That's when it's very challenging to
look at a company.

Stephen Peak, senior European fund manager at Henderson Touche Remnant

It doesn't make much difference whether a stock is on
AIM or the full list. What matters is the trading record and
the liquidity.

*Graham Shore, managing director of Shore Capital, investment management
group*

In the future, the best results will be obtained from solid investment (not speculation) in equities, gilts and long-term capital projects.
Nick Train, investment fund manager, M&G Group

Any sign of strength in the economy is liable to trigger a selloff in bonds which spills over into shares.
Quentin Lumsden

When judging a high-tech stock what matters is not just the underlying growth in product demand but also the company's ability to extract earnings from every dollar of those revenues.
Financial Times

If you pump enough money into the global economy something other than bonds and stocks will eventually rise in price.
Barry Riley, Financial Times

It is dangerous to assume that tired old blue chips in the portfolio will necessarily recover, some time. They may not. They may gently fade away.
Barry Riley, Financial Times

It is tempting for small companies to treat their size as an excuse. But ultimately companies are big because they are good, not the other way round.
Tony Jackson, Financial Times

Equities do not grow steadily. Even though the net result of bull and bear periods may be equivalent to a certain rate of growth, you can only be sure of this change in hindsight. Actual returns could differ widely from projections.
Krishna Guha, 'Weekend Money', Financial Times

Ever more money is being switched to back the winners, leaving a growing herd of also-rans to fumble along in the shadow of new stock market records.
Richard Waters, Financial Times

Historically, the share of equities in households' portfolios has risen as the proportion of over 35s in the workforce has risen, as it is this group which buys equities to prepare for retirement.
Investors Chronicle

Economics, as is so often the case in stock markets, might not necessarily be a reliable guide to the behaviour of sectors and stocks.
'Fund Manager', Investors Chronicle

I don't recommend internet stocks to people who don't like massive risk, especially at current levels. People are jumping into it like it's a gold rush.
Bill Gates, co-founder and chief executive of Microsoft

Growth Companies

The hallmark of a growth share is its ownership of lucrative revenue-creating assets allowing for expansion, often for decades, although just one piece of good news can transform a company's growth prospects. If you recognise a superb growth share before the crowd has spotted it, the world will think you are lucky but as my father often said, 'You make your own luck'.

Inevitably, small private investors have limited resources. However, this gives them a strong advantage because it is easier to find twelve super-stocks than it is to find one hundred.

What a company's stock sells for today, tomorrow or next week doesn't matter. What counts is how the company does over a five- or ten-year period.
Warren Buffett

If a company has increased earnings for fifteen years, it is probably just about to have a bad year.
Philip Carret, quoted in The New Money Masters *by John Train*

Growth requires a sacrifice of current profits to lay the foundations for worthwhile future improvement.
Philip Fisher

Keep paying attention to the near-term realities that will affect growth in earnings.
One Up on Wall Street, *Peter Lynch*

The very best way to make money in the market is in a small growth company that has been profitable for a couple of years and simply goes on growing.
Peter Lynch, quoted in The New Money Masters *by John Train*

We much prefer to buy the classic entrepreneurial story, where the guy has set it up in his garage and grown it.
John McClure, investment manager, Guinness Flight

Ten years ago, Glaxo was an extreme example of what we are after—a company whose prospects were not fully discovered.
Richard Peirson, head of UK equities at Framlington

The shares of those growth companies that are able to grow their earnings in this period of low growth will, at a terminal juncture, be valued on price-earnings ratios that many will now regard as unthinkable.
Nick Train, investment fund manager, M&G Group

My definition of a growth company is one that is capable of sustaining a premium return on its equity. Sustainable means this must have been achieved for at least five years.
Nick Train, investment fund manager, M&G Group

There are far fewer growth businesses out there than anyone believes—there are about 50 true growth businesses.
Nick Train

Wonder growth companies are not meant to stumble.
'Fund Manager', Investors Chronicle

Investments

Throughout their working lives, most people are financial magpies, collecting assorted investments in a piecemeal fashion. It surely must be better, I think, to collect a family of investments to prepare for all eventualities. But, as with your real family, your investment family cannot simply be left to fend for itself. If you nurture it with care, it will repay you handsomely.

Individuals who cannot master their emotions are ill-suited to profit from the investment process.
Benjamin Graham

Buy good securities, put them away, and forget them.
Timothy Bancroft, American financier

Start saving and investing early. It's a great habit to have.
Warren Buffett

With each investment you make, you should have the courage and the conviction to place at least ten per cent of your net worth in that stock.
Warren Buffett

Investing is most intelligent when it is most businesslike.
Benjamin Graham, founder of security analysis

Since the gold boom of the late 1970s, I cannot recall any investment theme that has caught investors' fancy on a global scale as much as the Asian emerging stock markets.
Dr Marc Faber

Never get rooted in an investment because of the feeling that it 'owes' you something.
The Zurich Axioms, Max Gunther

The game of professional investment is intolerably boring and over-exacting to anyone who is entirely exempt from the gambling instinct.
John Maynard Keynes

As time goes on, I get more and more convinced that the right method of investment is to put fairly large sums into enterprises which one thinks one knows something about and in management of which one thoroughly believes.
John Maynard Keynes, letter written in August 1934

It has always been possible in the past to notice new techniques or neglected areas of investment.
The New Money Masters, John Train

An attractive investment area must have favourable characteristics that should last five years or longer.
Ralph Wanger, quoted in The New Money Masters by John Train

Invest in inflation. It's the only thing going up.
Will Rogers

But a curiosity of human society, particularly in the investment field, is that humans will imitate each other.
Riding the Millennial Storm, *Nury Vittachi*

Investment, if you like, is a math exam where the powers that be work out the answers based on new formulae they develop after your papers have been handed in.
Dr Marc Faber quoted in Riding the Millennial Storm by Nury Vittachi

Well, since you're wanting to get people interested in the stock market in your country, we always say over here that ladies or girls, from birth to 18, they need good parents, from 18 to 30, they need good looks, from 30 to 50, a good personality. But after 50, you'd better have some good investments.
Ann Brewer (one of the Beardstown Ladies) to Bernice Cohen, in 'Mrs Cohen's Money' on Channel 4, May 1997

When I was a kid, it was common advice to buy a stock, put it in a vault, and forget about it. You don't hear that sort of concept anymore. We have lost confidence in the long term.
Michael Steinhardt, Steinhardt Partners

History shows that over the medium to long term, only asset-backed investments have the ability to deliver growth in both capital and income above the rate of inflation. This is vital because as people live longer so their investments have to last longer and achieve more.
An Introduction to Investments, *Legal & General*

Equity ownership, incidentally, also is very much a minority pursuit.
John Plender, Financial Times

However you look at it, the long term arguments in favour of equity investment are compelling.
Gillian O'Connor, FT Quarterly Review of Personal Finance

In the investment world those who do not have good ideas of their own can still profit by copying others.
Maggie Urry, Financial Times

It's a good rule not to invest in companies you don't follow.
Investors Chronicle

Investing is the action of placing overwhelming reliance on the quality of your target purchase—the underlying business.
Jeremy Utton, Analyst

Buying great businesses at fair prices is better than buying fair businesses at great prices.
Jeremy Utton, Analyst

Ageing baby boomers have bought everything there is to buy—they are now interested in investing. Right now there is this notion that the only way to plan for the long-term or save for retirement is equities.
Philip Roth, analyst at Dean Witter, New York

Never invest your money in anything that eats or needs repairing.
Billy Rose

10 Making The Gains

Having looked earlier at what the gurus and experts think about the process of buying and selling, values and prices, companies as investments, we are ready now to explore the theme of 'Making the Gains'. This is the pot of gold towards which all our efforts should be directed. It covers the gains, the profits and managing a portfolio.

Evidence shows that the largest gains come from investing early, rather than investing more, but later in life. Winston Churchill famously said, 'Saving is a very fine thing, especially when your parents have done it for you'.

A similar sentiment could begin to operate for investments, if today's investors pass on their winning portfolios to their children. It is hard to remember, but we are always looking for tomorrow's big winners, not today's. The real money is made by backing tomorrow's Coca-Colas when they are still small. It is not easy to make superb gains in a widely diversified portfolio with a large spread of shares. Private investors have an edge here, as they can rarely afford to invest in more than a dozen.

Gains

The reward is there for the taking; the only question is: Are you *conscious* enough to take it?
New Trading Dimensions, *Bill Williams*

How much is 10 per cent per month? Well, it is almost 300 per cent per year. A straight-line 10 per cent per month compounded would take a $10,000 account to over a million dollars in a bit more than four years. Has that been done? Absolutely, and it is being done even as you read this.
New Trading Dimensions, *Bill Williams*

To earn your money, you have to do the right thing.
Tony Dye, chief investment officer at Philips & Drew

The vast majority of the gains from diversification come with the first dozen or so stocks.
Investors Chronicle

Any share that holds up during market weakness is likely to be fast out of the traps in a recovery.
Fund Manager's Diary, Investors Chronicle

What the typical modern man desires to get with [money] is more money.
Bertrand Russell, twentieth-century philosopher

An industry that isn't a good return for investors can be a very important source of gains for a variety of downstream industries.
Paul Romer, economic theorist at the University of California at Berkeley

Profits

You may think gurus have advantages you cannot hope to match, but Warren Buffett, by far the world's most successful investor ever, lives miles away from the major financial centres of America and does not even use a simple calculator to decide which companies to invest in.

When you take the mystery out of stock market investing, your profits start to grow. Every extra year you leave your money invested moves the odds of a bigger profit outcome more in your favour. The big profits come from riding up the lengthy growth curve as it unfolds for a small growth company. George Soros has an evocative description for this. 'The way to build long-term returns is through preservation of capital and home runs'. American investors clearly appreciate baseball analogies. Everyone knows we should let the profits run, but in practice this is often hard to do. Persistence is a character trait all successful gurus have. They recognise that it may take many misses before you finally nail down the big winner.

They are equally adamant that the greatest returns come from concentrating your resources on just a few promising companies. Many stress the notion of targeting a few individual situations where you feel confident of the potential gains, then investing heavily in them. As Charles Munger, Warren Buffett's business partner of several decades, observes, 'You do better to make a few large bets and sit back and wait'. Paradoxically, financial commentators advise small private investors to 'spread the risk', but the investment gurus say just the opposite, 'concentrate your firepower on a few exceptionally good investments, to make superb profits'.

How should you resolve that paradox? I think novices and cautious investors should diversify, but as you gain more experience, hone in on the favourite shares you follow. Resorting to the imagery of a lion's kill, George Soros calls this, 'going for the throat'.

A fat wallet is the enemy of superior investment returns.
Warren Buffett

Business is all about putting out money today to get a
whole lot more back later.
Warren Buffett

Buying and selling each year, a stock that doubles in a
year for twenty years would turn $1,000 into $35,000
($22,000 after adjusting for tax). But making one single
investment of $1,000 that compounds at 100 per cent every
year for twenty years would create an investment worth
$1 million before tax.
Warren Buffett

An investor cannot earn superior profits from stocks
simply by committing to a specific category or style. He
can earn them only by carefully evaluating facts and
continuously exercising discipline.
Warren Buffett

No one ever makes a loss by taking a profit.
Dr Marc Faber

To achieve satisfactory investment results is easier than
most people realise; to achieve superior results is harder
than it looks.
The Intelligent Investor, *Benjamin Graham*

The Engine which drives Enterprise is not
Thrift, but Profit.
Treatise on Money, *John Maynard Keynes*

The biggest profits come from sitting, not trading.
Jesse Livermore

It is never your thinking that makes big money,
it's the sitting.

Jesse Livermore

If seven out of ten stocks perform as expected, that's good
going ... but six out of ten is all it takes to produce a very
favourable return.

One Up on Wall Street, Peter Lynch

Things are never clear in the stock market and by the time
they are, it is too late to profit from them.

One Up on Wall Street, Peter Lynch

It only takes a handful of big winners to make a lifetime of
investing worthwhile.

One Up on Wall Street, Peter Lynch

The best results flow from a progression of surprises.

Peter Lynch, quoted in The New Money Masters by John Train

When the news seems terrible, that's when you make the
big money in the market.

Peter Lynch, quoted in The New Money Masters by John Train

Buy shares to make profits, not to preserve capital.

One Up on Wall Street, Peter Lynch

I knew from being a poker player that you have to bet
heavily when you've got huge odds in your favour.

Charlie Munger, business partner to Warren Buffett

The objective is to buy a non-dividend paying stock that
compounds for thirty years at 15% a year and pay only a
single tax of 35% at the end of the period.

Charlie Munger

I am convinced that every dollar a young man saves, properly invested, will return him twenty over the course of his life.
Investment Biker, *Jim Rogers*

My philosophy has always been to be profitable every single month. I even try to be profitable every single day.
Marty Schwartz, independent futures trader

One of the best ways to increase profits is to do goal setting and visualisations in order to align the conscious and subconscious with making profits.
Ed Seykota, futures trader

Don't worry about missing the first 10 per cent of the rise (when you have bought while the index is low)—the ultimate gain will be substantial.
Jim Slater

It's not whether you're right or wrong that's important, but how much money you make when you're right and how much you lose when you're wrong.
George Soros

If you look back at the whole of the 1980s and at the hundreds of days the market was open, most of the market's good performance was concentrated on a few dozen days. Missing those vital good—but unpredictable—days would ruin a fund's performance.
Philip Brown, chief investment officer at Meridian Investment Company

The way to build long-term returns is through preservation of capital and home runs.
George Soros

To buy when others are despondently selling and to sell when others are greedily buying requires the greatest fortitude and pays the greatest reward.

Sir John Templeton

Nervous investors may want to take their profits now while the market is at record highs and come back in again after any correction. But if you are brave enough to sit it out, statistics show that you will reap the rewards.

Ian Millward, of Chase de Vere, August 1997

After all, who needs to *beat* the index? In the year to August 31, the market rose 10 per cent—enough to satisfy all but the greediest investor.

James Macintosh, Financial Times

The way to outperform is not to chase the index but to try to anticipate changes in investment trends by concentrating on sectors or regions that are expected to grow in importance.

Ian Orton, Financial Times

History teaches us that it is very easy to exaggerate the dangers surrounding equities. These have posted huge returns in the past eighty years precisely because investors' worst fears have not materialised.

Investors Chronicle

The most profits come from recognising the right themes, not by saying where the Dow will be.

Robert J. Farrell

Most of the time, it seems impossible to spot a change of trend in an underlying share price in advance, so we end up jumping on trends once they have become established. Often that proves profitable.

'Fund Manager', Investors Chronicle

No one can be sure what the returns will be on any form of savings over the next forty years. If inflation stays low and economic growth stays subdued, today's relatively low long-term interest rates and high share prices point to far lower returns on securities than over the past twenty-three years.

Graham Searjeant, The Times

When a share price goes up rapidly, people think there's a bid in the background; but if they follow the profits they will see these are going up at roughly the same speed as the share price.

David Franks, managing director, Regent Inns

Don't talk about 5% or 10% profit improvements. I always want to double profits every two or three years. You get a completely different thought process by aiming for targets like that.

Charles Allen, chief executive at Granada plc

Portfolios

When you have savings in the bank or other investments, whether you realise it or not, you have become a fund manager in charge of your own portfolio of funds. When it comes to investing for your own financial security, the buck really does stop with you. There is no doubt that with good planning and a little 'know-how' your share portfolio can produce a genuine nest egg. Investing early in a rising market makes a huge impact on the speed at which that portfolio grows.

From comments made by many successful gurus it is clear that portfolio-builders invest for the long term and are psychologically more willing to ride out the dips. John Maynard Keynes said of long-term investing, 'It seems to me to be most important not to be upset out of one's permanent holdings by being too attentive to market movements'. This brilliant 1930s economist reputedly had stunning successes with his portfolio of well-chosen long-term shares, but made most of his killings as a currency speculator when rates were floating during the inter-war period.

I would say that if our predictions have been a little better than other people's it's because we've tried to make fewer of them.
Charlie Munger

When we bought something and ran out of money, we would look at the portfolio and push out whatever appeared to be the least attractive item at that point.
Jim Rogers' on his early years in the Quantum Fund with George Soros

I now realise that achieving above average returns is not merely a matter of which stock you pick, but also how you structure your portfolio.
The Warren Buffett Portfolio, *Robert G. Hagstrom*

There is a lot of churning rather than genuine sector rotation. If you had the right portfolio over the past three months, you had the wrong one this week.

Paul O'Connor, strategist at Credit Suisse First Boston

The ideal investment portfolio is divided between the purchase of really secure future income (where future appreciation or depreciation will depend on the rate of interest) and equities which one believes to be capable of a large improvement to offset the fairly numerous cases which, with the best skill in the world, will go wrong.

John Maynard Keynes

We spend a lot of time positioning the portfolio for increasing interest rates. Of course, a bolt from the blue can cause a correction, but increasing interest rates are more likely to cause a fall.

Tony Robinson, global equity strategist with Lombard Odier International Portfolio Management Ltd

The argument for trackers is pretty strong. Over the long term, it is pretty hard to beat them.

Phillip Warland, chief executive, Autif (Association of Unit Trusts and Investment Funds)

And the more people diversify their portfolios overseas, the less diversification these outflows deliver. The strategy is inherently self-defeating when it ceases to be a strictly minority pursuit.

Leader article, Financial Times, *April 1999*

If you are using a tracker as a core holding in a balanced portfolio, you want the fund that most closely matches the index over time.

'Weekend Money', Financial Times

In a slow-moving economy, growth is not going to pop up conveniently in your portfolio. You are going to have to seek it out—and weed out the dogs.
Barry Riley, Financial Times

Even for the most risk-averse investor, an optimum portfolio can contain far fewer stocks than you might think.
Investors Chronicle

The humble tracker has much to recommend it.
Investors Chronicle

New readers must trade on paper for a few months before exposing themselves to the stress of using real money.
'The Options Trader', Investors Chronicle

The popularity of index tracking funds rests on the fact that investors are either unwilling or unable to differentiate between the skills of active fund managers.
Graham Harrison, Asset Risk Consultancy

Investors in trackers are saying that they are prepared to accept market average performance, safe in the knowledge that there is no risk of serious underperformance.
Graham Harrison, Asset Risk Consultancy

11 Invest or Speculate?

· ·

It may seem odd that the penultimate theme, 'Invest or Speculate' takes an in-depth look at investors and speculators. They surely should have been covered at a much earlier stage. However, I feel that the techniques and skills of investing are preliminary topics to explore fully before we turn to what investors and speculators actually do or should do. As in every previous theme, comments by the gurus give insights into why their proven techniques have given them such resounding success.

Essentially, I think there are only two kinds of investors: the successful ones, and everyone else. If you want to be a seriously rich investor, first you must learn how to survive in the market. The switchback ride that markets pursue can provoke a stream of conflicting emotions in even the most tranquil person. Elaine Gazarelli, a top Wall Street analyst for eleven years, makes this telling comment about confused investor emotion, 'I do the opposite to what I feel I should do. When I'm sick in my stomach, it's time to buy. When I feel great, it's time to sell'.

Perhaps Warren Buffett is an exception, but another brilliant stock-picker was the epitome of a self-taught long-term investor and, hence, an inspiration to others hoping to emulate her dazzling example. Anne Scheiber, a spinster whose one obsessive hobby was investing, lived to be 101 years old. Over fifty years, from 1944 to 1994, this retired tax office auditor, who earned no more than $4,400 per year, turned an initial investment of $5,000 into $22 million. The original $5,000 was the lump sum element in her pension package. If she had simply tried to track the performance of a popular US stock market index like the Standard & Poor's 500 index, her $5,000 would only have grown to $726,849.

Anne Scheiber's story illustrates many investor truisms. Hence, small investors may start small, but they do not have to think small. Her record shows professionals do not have a monopoly on investment skills. If you decide to be a long-term investor, like Anne Scheiber you can ride out the peaks and troughs of unpredictable market activity. She invested right through the 1960s and 1970s when the US market was sluggish and sat through the 1987 October crash. In a panic, long-term investors can profit if they fix their sights on the good stories of the shares they are holding. Throughout her incredibly lengthy investment career, she rarely sold any shares. Therefore, after thirty or so years, she was the owner of many companies that generated excellent cash flows and paid her a rising dividend stream. Her example suggests that buying good blue chip shares and holding them long term pays rich dividends for patient investors—but it clearly helps if, like Anne Scheiber, you live to be 101! I was once asked what was the point of her making so much money when she was a spinster and lived very frugally. The punchline was that she donated her portfolio to a college for women and because the funds went to charity, her stingy employer, the American Internal Revenue Service (the tax authority), did not make a penny out of it.

Investors
....

Market pessimism is the ally of the fundamental investor
for the bargains it provides.
Warren Buffett

An investor only has to do a small number of
things right and avoid making major mistakes to be
outstandingly successful.
Warren Buffett

We just focus on a few outstanding companies. We're
focus investors.
Warren Buffett

By periodically investing in an index [tracker] fund, the
know-nothing investor can actually outperform most
investment professionals.
Warren Buffett

If you are a know-something investor, able to understand
business economics and to find five to ten sensibly priced
companies that possess important long-term competitive
advantages, conventional diversification (broadly based
active portfolios) makes no sense to you.
Warren Buffett

As an investor, he has discipline, patience, flexibility,
courage, confidence and decisiveness.
Peter Lynch, on Warren Buffett

I have never seen a boom during which investors didn't
ardently believe that foreigners would drive prices higher.
Dr Marc Faber

Investor reaction to falling prices doesn't seem to change. A bad experience leads them to back off and to avoid the entire asset class in which they have lost money. They continue to avoid it, no matter how good its value becomes.
Dr Marc Faber

Many minds make a market but your job (as an investor) is to be 'smarter than the average investor'.
Philip Fisher

An investor's worst enemy is not the stock market but oneself.
Benjamin Graham

Everyone has the brain power to make money in stocks. Not everyone has the stomach.
Peter Lynch

The law of averages, if you are better than the average investor, must infallibly pull you farther and farther ahead.
Peter Lynch, quoted in The New Money Masters *by John Train*

With enough shrewdness, fanaticism and discipline [investors will beat the market].
Charles Munger, Warren Buffett's business partner

Most investors are not able to find good information and advice. Many, if they had sound advice, would not follow it.
William O'Neil

Individual investors worry too much about taxes and commissions. Your key objective should be to first make a net profit.
William O'Neil

Most investors cannot look at stocks objectively. They are always hoping and having favourites, and they rely on their hopes and personal opinions rather than paying attention to the opinion of the marketplace, which is more frequently right.
William O'Neil

In a crowded room, you only have to see one inch above everyone else to notice things that others will miss. It is this extra inch the active investor is striving to achieve.
Jim Slater

It is obvious that the average person is not going to beat stockbrokers, merchant bankers and other professionals at their own game right across the board. The only way the lay investor can stand a chance will be by the selection of a small part of the board and concentration of available spare time in becoming relatively expert in that small area.
Jim Slater, Analyst, September 1990

The investor, unlike the speculator, does not have to worry too much about the short term.
John Train

Investors operate with limited funds and limited intelligence: They do not need to know everything.
George Soros, quoted in The New Money Masters *by John Train*

A surprising number of the greatest investors develop a new approach, like an art collector who finds and exploits an overlooked category.
The New Money Masters, *John Train*

I'm not in Wall Street for my health.
J.P. Morgan

The secret to success in the market lies not in discovering some incredible indicator or elaborate theory: rather, it lies within each individual.

The New Market Wizards, *Jack D. Schwager*

My money never leaves the Street [Wall Street]. It's the best place for it to be.

Pat Bologne, shoe-shine boy at 60 Wall Street during the 1920s. He invested $5,000 and salvaged $1,700 in the 1929 October crash

The investor is always portrayed as a person who goes from extreme confidence to sheer panic. A look at the way any stock market moves reveals the accuracy of this portrait—soaring markets do not level off, but rise vertically and then fall vertically. Spikes are the norm, not the exception.

Riding the Millennial Storm, *Nury Vittachi*

Perhaps the most important change is that the world has become much more short-term oriented. All sorts of people who used to be investors are now traders.

Michael Steinhardt, Steinhardt Partners

In the 1950s and 1960s, the heroes were the long-term investors; today, the heroes are the wise guys.

Michael Steinhardt, Steinhardt Partners

It is a common failing among investors to let enthusiasm control their cheque books. Many dive into a company's shares and are disappointed when they fail to perform.

Charles Wyatt

Investor psychology is not to sell while the market is whizzing down, but instead to bail out when their funds are back to the level where they started.

John Authers, 'Weekend Money', Financial Times

When different types of investors dominate, incompatible views can hold sway.
Barry Riley, 'Weekend Money', Financial Times

Investors are especially vulnerable, however, when they simply chase dreams.
Barry Riley, 'Weekend Money', Financial Times

Minor changes in the assumptions by investors about growth can have very large effects on share prices.
Barry Riley, Financial Times

Investors must avoid the trap of valuing today's businesses by yesterday's standards.
Peter Martin, Financial Times

It signifies the greed of people—they are willing time and again to suspend their rational judgement in the hope that someone (an active fund manager) has that magic touch.
Pattie Dunn, chairman of Barclays Global Investors, the world's largest institutional fund manager

My approach to traded options is to concentrate on tactics and let the broad sweep of strategy develop out of the behaviour of investors themselves.
'Traded Options', Investors Chronicle

Every stock market guru has maxims by which he lives his investment life.
Investors Chronicle

Don't move all your money in a hasty manner. Investors should determine how much income they need to generate and move only what they have to protect. It would be crazy to go from 100% equity holdings to cash.
Ian Beauchamp, director and chief economist at Hambros Fund Management

You can tell a successful investor by the companies he keeps.

Jeremy Utton, editor of Analyst

Pension fund managers have to take the long view, but seeing things in a historical perspective is also sound advice for private investors.

Dominick Coyle, FT Quarterly Review of Personal Finance

Investment trusts find it easy to ignore shareholders' interests until they come under attack from predators, which can quickly rally unhappy shareholders.

Roger Taylor, 'Weekend Money', Financial Times

Investors must beware—this year's fashion can quickly become next year's tank top.

Justin Urquhart Stewart, Barclays Stockbrokers

One of the most robust laws of experimental psychology is that individuals are wildly inconsistent in the way they rank rewards over time, and place a heavy emphasis on rewards in the present.

Playing the Game—The Takeover, *Will Hutton*

People love mutuality, but not as much as a cheque for £600.

Spokesperson for Alliance & Leicester Building Society

Every rock'n'roll person has to have a keen financial brain, even the ones you least suspect.

Bob Geldof

Almost every American would sooner get 80 per cent from a risky investment than 4 per cent from a safe one. The consequence is that there are frequent losses of money and continual worry and fret.

Bertrand Russell, the great twentieth-century philosopher

Speculators

Successful speculation during the upswing of a bubble looks deceptively easy, astonishingly rewarding and incredibly fast. Needless to say, success in this endeavour requires that you pay even more attention to preparation and research. As Bill Williams claims, only 3 per cent of traders are successful, while the rest are consistent losers. I do not speculate, but investors can learn much from the wisdom of the few successful investors who choose to share their expertise with us. Jesse Livermore and Joseph Kennedy were both famous as Wall Street's most successful speculators during the first two decades of the twentieth century. They reputedly made a fortune during the great October crash of 1929 by selling stocks short. (This involved selling shares they did not own in the hope of being able to buy them back later at a lower price).

As a student of human nature, I have always felt that a good speculator should be able to tell what a man will do with his money before he does it.
Bernard Baruch, American financier and statesman

Basic economic theory suggests that demand falls as prices go up. But in the case of speculative markets, the opposite seems to be true.
Dr Marc Faber

The multitude speculates in options too much because they think it is a way to get rich quick.
William O'Neil

Professionals and speculators are not primarily concerned with making superior long-term forecasts but with for-seeing changes in the conventional basis of valuation a short time ahead of the general public.
John Maynard Keynes

Speculators may do no harm as bubbles on the steady stream of enterprise. But the position is serious when enterprise becomes the bubble on the whirlpool of speculation.
John Maynard Keynes

Professionals and speculators … are concerned with how the market will value an investment under the influences of mass psychology, three months or a year hence.
John Maynard Keynes

Once you get a game going like this with the central banks you know speculators using leverage are also going to follow.
Frank Leitner, trader

All the money we dealt with was unreal: abstract numbers which flashed across the trading pit with a flurry of hands.
Nick Leeson, the trader who reputedly brought about the demise of Barings Bank

Unlike industrial metals which are actually used up, gold is a speculative football.
John Train, chairman of Montrose Advisors, investment managers in New York City

One of the most reliable symptoms of a boom coming to an end is the sight of speculators focusing on a few issues, usually in just one sector.
Riding the Millennial Storm, *Nury Vittachi*

Once the speculative tide starts running, few can resist its pull.
John Train

First-time speculators want to make a killing in the market. They want too much, too fast, without doing the necessary study and preparation or acquiring the essential methods and skills.
William O'Neil

The speculator can choose to only bet when the odds are in his favour. That is an important positional advantage.
Larry Hite, Mint Investment Management Company

The entire global equities investing scene itself had become one huge speculative excess. The crash was coming. It had to.
Riding the Millennial Storm, Nury Vittachi

Speculating about unexpected events can pay off.
Byron Wein, Morgan Stanley

Speculative bubbles are observationally equivalent to movements in unobserved factors ... It is impossible to verify the existence of asset-price bubbles.
Tim Cogley, economist at the San Francisco Federal Reserve Board

There's no one-way rise in foreign exchange. In the short-term, the market moves on speculation and player's positions. However, long-term movements can only be gauged from (economic) fundamentals.
Eishi Wakabayashi, executive vice-president of Kankaku Securities (America)

An investment is a speculation that didn't work out.
Popular saying on Wall Street

October. This is one of the peculiarly dangerous months to speculate in stocks. The others are July, January, September, April, November, May, March, June, December, August and February.
Mark Twain

Fund Managers as Investors

The law of supply and demand is more important than all the analyst opinions on Wall Street.
William O'Neil

A large number of UK investment managers do not have formal qualifications, do not read extensively about investment theory and have little time for reflective thinking as they are mainly news driven.
Jim Slater, letter to Investors Chronicle, *22 March 1996*

The idea that stock-jobbers have secret sources of information and … mark the prices of their wares up and down accordingly is of course, moonshine. They take the same interest in public affairs as the rest of us, no more, no less, and have the same sources of information, which is usually the press.
Lawrence Jones, a merchant banker in 1914.

12 Winning Wisdom

••••••••••••••••••••••••••••••••••••

Compiling this *Treasury* has given me much pleasure. I hope it will be as inspirational for readers as it has been for me. I hugely enjoy sifting and sorting through my vast array of quotations and am constantly searching for more. It seems only right that the final theme should cover the essence of success. It includes not only success itself, but the skill of contrarianism, which is a classic route most gurus use to achieve magnificent results. We have already seen under earlier themes, that several gurus are out-standing contrarians.

Here, I would like to share with you three thoughts that sum up my personal attitude to successful investing:

- Start to think like a long-term investor and very soon you will find you are behaving like one.
- For investors, wealth isn't something to admire: it is something to create.
- When you find a group of companies that you are happy to hold for years, you have reached Utopia for private investors.

Success
••••••••••••••

It is an old cliché that nothing succeeds like success. Repeatedly, the experience of the gurus reveals that success is possible with a modest research effort, if you stay focused on those opportunities that offer the greatest chance of outstanding success. You do not need the expertise of a qualified accountant to make an unqualified success of your investments, but if you can master your own strengths and weaknesses as an investor, you have probably won the hardest battle and if you study your successes, you may be able to repeat them.

Sadly, however, you may know how to make a successful investment without ever being able to do it. But if you can accept the outlay of time, effort and expense as your first investments on the road to success, you will not begrudge the costs. Keep fine tuning your portfolio, to ensure you have the greatest prospects of making profits from the few shares you are holding, because to succeed, you need only be right more often than you are wrong.

Yet, if at first you don't succeed, don't worry as you're just like the rest of us. In 1921, Walt Disney founded the Laugh-O-Gram Corporation in Kansas City. When his backers pulled out, he declared bankruptcy and took off for Hollywood, with just one suitcase of clothes.

Following the professionals is no guarantee of success but the gurus have many words of wisdom to illuminate your path. Their diversity shows there are almost as many routes to investment success as there are successful investors.

To be successful, you should concentrate on the world of companies, not arcane accountancy mathematics.
Warren Buffett

The stock market is like a game of stud poker:
as long as the cards suggest favourable odds of
success, stay with the hand.
Peter Lynch

I was broke in the 1970s, and I never want to be broke
again. My philosophy was that if you make money every
month, nothing bad is going to happen to you.
Marty Schwartz, independent futures trader

I always try to encourage people that are thinking of
going into this business. I tell them, 'Think that you might
become more successful than you ever dreamt, because
that's what happened to me'.
Marty Schwartz, independent futures trader

I became a winning trader when I was able to say,
'To hell with my ego, making money is more important.'
Marty Schwartz, independent futures trader

Back individuals with good original ideas, products
or marketing, a decent record and an unsated appetite
to succeed.
Graham Searjeant, The Times

One key to success in international investment is to
recognise the value of sitting tight.
William Essex, The Sunday Times

Paradoxically, the way to do well in the short term is to
aim for long-term success.
Quentin Lumsden, editor, Quantum Leap

My secret of success is never to get excited when things go
right or depressed when they go badly.
Tim Martin, managing director of JD Wetherspoon

Success comes from focusing in on what you really like and are good at—not challenging every random thing.
Bill Gates, co-founder and chief executive of Microsoft

Americans celebrate success. We envy it.
Mike Blackburn, ex-chief executive of Halifax Group

The more I practise, the luckier I get.
Stephen Riley, chief executive, Denby Pottery

If people have a true interest in something they have more chance of succeeding.
John Haynes, chairman of Haynes Publishing

Success comes from attention to detail and doing everything well.
Maurice Bennett, managing director of Oasis Stores

Once I have made up my mind, I screen out everything except what will make it succeed.
Napoleon

Nothing corrupts faster than success.
Lafayette, Hero of Two Worlds, *Olivier Bernier*

When in doubt, do what someone successful does.
Suze Orman

Contrarians

Contrary thinkers do not invest because prices are falling. They buy when good shares have become outstanding bargains.

It seems to be astonishingly difficult to buy when the price is low and sell when it is high, because it demands a contrary view. It takes tremendous nerve to buy as a panic reaches its height, but buying then can bring amazing gains.

———————————

The general idea is that what works most of the time is nearly the opposite of what works in the long run.
William Eckhardt, futures trader

The central principle of investment is to go contrary to the general opinion, on the grounds that if everyone agreed about its merits, the investment is inevitably too dear and therefore unattractive.
John Maynard Keynes

When I see hysteria, I usually look to see if I shouldn't be going the other way.
Jim Rogers

Just about every time you go against panic, you will be right if you can stick it out.
Jim Rogers

Using contrary thinking is investment at its best and will beat any system. On paper it may seem easy but in practice it is very difficult and requires considerable nerve.
Jim Slater, Analyst, September 1990

There is a very important difference between being a theoretical contrarian and dealing with it in practical terms.
Michael Steinhardt, Steinhardt Partners

In order to win as a contrarian, you need the right timing and you have to put on a position in the appropriate size.
Michael Steinhardt, Steinhardt Partners

'Buy when there's blood in the streets.' Easy to say, but utterly contrary to one's instincts: so much of good investment is counter-intuitive.
John Train, Financial Times

The trick is not being a contrarian, but being a contrarian at the right time.
Market Wizards, *Jack D. Schwager*

You can't be a successful contrarian by just using sentiment, survey numbers or other measures of bullish consensus.
Market Wizards, *Jack D. Schwager*

The successful contrarian needs to be able to filter out the best opportunities.
Market Wizards, *Jack D. Schwager*

I do the opposite to what I feel I should do. When I'm sick in my stomach, it's time to buy. When I feel great, it's time to sell.
Elaine Gazarelli, top Wall Street analyst for eleven years

Good contrarians should always be betting against the conventional wisdom.
Philip Coggan, Financial Times

Trade against the ruling mood—but let the mood have a good run first.
Anthony Harris, Financial Times

Markets do not rise when everyone is bullish, quite the opposite. The more bears I can find at present, the happier I am with my strategy.
'Options Trader', Investors Chronicle

If you buy the same securities as other people, you will have the same results as other people. It is impossible to produce a superior performance unless you do something different from the majority.

Sir John Templeton

I believe it is critical not to be part of the herd when investing in financial markets. Just because most investors are moving in a particular direction doesn't make it the best direction. In fact, often it has meant the opposite.

Jeffrey Vinik, when manager of the world's largest mutual fund, Fidelity's Magellan fund

Whenever the consensus in the investment world starts to pronounce something, you can be sure the opposite is about to happen.

David Roche, president of Independent Strategy, a global investment research consultancy

If you make the same 'correct' investment decision as everybody else you will only make a small profit. All that money being invested by other people will have pushed the price up by the time you get there.

William Essex, The Sunday Times

Wealth

Prosperity is not just money in the bank, it is an attitude of mind. It seems no accident that success and prosperity should march together, hand in hand. Masters in every human skill have exhibited how indivisible these twin attributes can be. Here are Van Gogh's intimate musings on the link, writing (in Letter 605) to his beloved younger brother Theo, early in 1890, the last year of his life. 'I can already see the day coming when I shall enjoy a measure of success and long for the solitude and the sad life I lead here, gazing through the iron bars of the cell at the reaper in the field. Misfortune does have its uses. To have success and lasting prosperity, one must be of a different disposition than I am; I shall never accomplish what I ought to have wanted, ought to have striven for!' In May 1999, almost 109 years after his untimely death, a rare item of Van Gogh's later works that is still in private hands fetched $19.8 million (£12 million, including the auctioneer's premium), in a Christie's sale in New York. What, I wonder, would Van Gogh have made of that!

Uniqueness can be astonishingly rewarding, but the experience of the gurus convincingly shows that investing in the stock market is one of the best routes to creating long-term wealth for ordinary mortals. To build real wealth, therefore, savers must turn themselves into investors. In Britain, about 34 million people have yet to discover the wealth-creating equities bonanza. If you buy a sound portfolio of company shares, its growth over the years will be the powerhouse of your future wealth. Every private investor should make a lifetime commitment to create wealth by taking that route.

When I was a child, it became a family game to watch me at mealtimes because I always left a morsel of my favourite part of the meal to the last. The game was to guess in advance what that last mouthful would be. It seems entirely fitting to apply this little quirk to the *Treasury* and end on the topic of wealth. Not because it is the dearest thing to my heart, but because I now realise it is the best passport to a liberated life, as long as you retain your sense of values.

I see no shame for people today to want to be wealthy, especially if they use their own efforts and ingenuity to achieve it. What I have discovered is that when you have created your own nest egg, your 'circle of financial security' if you like, being magnanimous with your money is a tremendous spin-off. As the age-old saying goes; to be born a millionaire is lucky, to become one takes hard work, but if you die one, you're a fool. Napoleon observed, 'Riches do not consist in the possession of treasures but in the use made of them.' But we'll let the gurus have the last words on wealth.

Bill (Gates) and I both have a similar philosophy on giving back to our communities. I know in my case that 99-plus per cent of my wealth (currently about $18 billion) will go back to society, because we have been treated extraordinarily well by society.
Warren Buffett

The secret has been out for fifty years but I have seen no trend towards value investing in the thirty-five years I've practiced it. There seems to be some perverse human characteristic that makes easy things difficult.
Warren Buffet

The Asian crisis has left me shell shocked. I have never read of, or seen, such a total economic breakdown and massive destruction of wealth as has occurred, against all expectations, in Asia in the last six months.
Dr Marc Faber, 'Gloom, Boom & Doom Report', February 1998

In the next ten to twenty years, the changes we are going to see in terms of new centres of wealth will be mind-boggling. Only investors who understand this will be able to capitalise on the changes.

Dr Marc Faber

I think mutual funds are an absolutely outstanding way to invest. I believe every person should own their own home, own real estate, and have an individual stock account or own mutual funds. Those are the only ways you can make any substantial income above your salary.

William O'Neil

When I came to New York in 1968, I was a poor boy from Alabama. By 1979, I had made more money than I knew existed in the world.

Jim Rogers

It requires a great deal of boldness and a great deal of caution to make a great fortune.

N.M. Rothschild

The key to building wealth is to preserve capital and wait patiently for the right opportunity to make the extraordinary gains.

Victor Sperandeo

I always laugh at people who say, 'I've never met a rich technician.' I love that! It is such an arrogant, nonsensical response. I used fundamentals for nine years and got rich as a technician.

Marty Schwartz, independent futures trader

Fund managers do not create wealth. We trade it around.

Pattie Dunn, chairman of Barclays Global Investors, the world's largest institutional fund manager

Trading is likely the most exciting way to make a living and/or accumulate a fortune. You are your own boss and your own worst enemy.
New Trading Dimensions, *Bill Williams*

We all know about wealth generation, and we as a society talk about it endlessly—but we brush aside the merest intrusive thought about wealth destruction, refusing to acknowledge that it is as inevitable as its sunnier counterpart.
Riding the Millennial Storm, *Nury Vittachi*

Extreme wealth will always trigger moral indignation.
Bronwen Maddox, Financial Times

For it was observable in the famous South Sea year [1720], when so many immense fortunes were suddenly gained, and as suddenly lost, that more people lost their wits from the prodigious flow of unexpected riches, than from the entire loss of their whole substance.
William Cullen, Scottish physician, (1710 to 1790)

Riches do not consist in the possession of treasures but in the use made of them.
Napoleon

Final Thought!

There is only one long-range financial plan you need, and that is the intention to get rich.
The Zurich Axioms, *Max Gunther*

Favourite Quotes

www.mrscohen.com

I am building a Mrs Cohen community for people who want to improve their finances.

If you would like to join, visit my website: www.mrscohen.com

You can read my stockmarket diary and my views on major company announcements and receive helpful advice to guide you through the complicated world of the stockmarket and personal finance.

Why not enter your favourite investment quotations on the site? Senders of the three I like most will each receive a free copy of whichever of my books they would like to own. Simply click on Mrs Cohen's Quotations and enter the code 10990001.

I find making my money work is a fascinating and rewarding hobby. Let me and my team show you how it's done.